EVERYTHING
IS
WRONG
WITH YOU

EVERYTHING
IS
WRONG
WITH YOU

THE MODERN WOMAN'S GUIDE TO FINDING SELF-CONFIDENCE THROUGH SELF-LOATHING

WENDY MOLYNEUX

TOW BOOKS

Cincinnati, Ohio
www.towbooks.com

12 11 10 09 08   5 4 3 2 1

Distributed in Canada by Fraser Direct, 100 Armstrong Avenue, Georgetown, ON, Canada L7G 5S4, Tel: (905) 877-4411; Distributed in the U.K. and Europe by David & Charles, Brunel House, Newton Abbot, Devon, TQ12 4PU, England, Tel: (+44) 1626 323200, Fax: (+44) 1626 323319, E-mail: postmaster@davidandcharles.co.uk; Distributed in Australia by Capricorn Link, P.O. Box 704, Windsor, NSW 2756 Australia, Tel: (02) 4577-3555

Library of Congress Cataloging-in-Publication Data

Molyneux, Wendy.

  Everything is wrong with you : the modern woman's guide to finding self-confidence through self-loathing / by Wendy Molyneux. -- 1st edition.

    p. cm.

  ISBN 978-1-58297-535-1 (pbk. : alk. paper)

  1. Conduct of life--Humor. 2. Self-help techniques--Humor. 3. Women--Humor. I. Title.

  PN6231.C6142M64 2008

  818'.602--dc22

                                                                    2007035052

Edited by John Warner and Jane Friedman
Cover and interior designed by Claudean Wheeler
Illustrations by Wainscot Turkney, Joshua Roflow,
    and Claudean Wheeler
Production coordinated by Mark Griffin

F+W PUBLICATIONS, INC.

TABLE OF CONTENTS

$\mathcal{I}$ntroduction

As an enlightened modern female with a fantastic career, handsome husband, tastefully furnished home, and well-behaved pets, I initially set out to write a book about how you, my female contemporaries, could attempt to emulate me. But then, while sitting in my doctor's office, I happened to pick up a few women's magazines and look through them. After just a few short minutes I realized that I am not, in fact, as awesome as I imagined.

Here I was, gloating, thinking I had something to share with the world, but like a fool I had not even noticed that I had gone too long without washing my makeup brushes. A few more minutes of reading and I realized I was not pleasing my husband in bed, had flabby triceps, and was not making use of the best self-tanners. I owned no formal shorts, was not eating enough pomegranates, and couldn't remember the last time I disinfected the crisper in my refrigerator. I hadn't given my bedroom a "summer makeover," my friends had not received cards that I made by hand from cut paper and wood stamps, and I had never, ever bleached my butthole.

In short, it became clear that I had been focusing on the wrong things.

And so I went home and immediately threw out the five-hundred-page book I had already written, which was entitled *I'm Perfect Just the Way I Am—Join Me!*, and started from scratch. Clearly, if we were perfect, there wouldn't be an entire industry churning out magazines month after month to help us. We aren't better than we think we are—we're much, much worse. Obviously, these gentle magazine editors aren't in this for the money! They want to help us. They know that the only way to be empowered is to be completely disempowered. It's like when the U.S. government wanted to empower the Iraqi people by going into their country and taking over. Only by getting rid of their power, and, metaphorically, pointing out the cellulite on their thighs and the ancient sectarian feuds on their buttocks, are we able to build them back up again.

And so, while other self-help books will try to tell you there's nothing wrong with you, I'm here to tell you that *everything* is wrong with you.

That's right. The problem isn't that you lack self-confidence; it's that you have too much! You are sailing along, thinking that being a size-eight woman with a six-figure career is good enough. Meanwhile, a size-four woman with a seven-figure career is boning your husband and abducting your baby.

Should you panic? Yes, absolutely.

But!

The good news is that if you read this book and put my advice into action, you will not only become the perfect woman—impeccably dressed, well-spoken, well-married, great at entertaining and the sexual arts, and the mother of a brood of exemplary children—you will also become a highly skilled ninja![1]

Am I promising a lot? Yes. But that is what this country is about: making empty promises in order to acquire a vast personal fortune. And if you think that's wrong, I guess maybe you should just get in a time machine and go back to Communist Russia or whatever. I guess you think it would be fun to work in a spoon factory twelve hours a day and stand in line for bread and die of exhaustion at seventeen.

Jesus, what's wrong with you?

Seriously, what *is* wrong with you? Again—and I'm only saying this because I love you—*everything*.

Including:

  1. Your hair

---

[1] You will not become a highly skilled ninja.

2. Your clothes

3. The way you stand

4. Your body

5. Your taste in music

6. Your ability to spot vampires walking among us

7. Your relationships with your family

8. Your relationships with men

9. Your relationships with woodland creatures, including:
   a. Dolphins
   b. Bears
   c. Lions
   d. Monkeys, regular
   e. Monkeys, talking
   f. Monkeys, musical
   g. Babies

10. Your belief that it's OK just to be yourself

11. Your dancing skills

12. Your understanding of proto-modernist poetry, particularly that of Emily Dickinson and Walt Whitman

13. Your conception that Dickinson did not have an aesthetic but was just a "crazy bitch who lived in an attic"

14. Your statement that Whitman was "weird" and smelled like "tabaccy"

15. The fact that you clearly did not do any of the reading for this class

16. Please see me during my office hours to discuss

As you can see, we have quite a task ahead of us. So grab a cup of coffee and a snack—Kidding! No eating!—and let's get to work. After all, if our government was able to bring total peace and calm to the Middle East, there's hope for you yet!

Chapter 1

YOU'RE LONELY

~ or ~

I'M JUST NOT THAT INTO YOU

~ or ~

IT'S NOT WHAT YOU'RE DATING, IT'S WHAT'S DATING YOU

CAN FAIRY TALES COME TRUE?

As little girls, we were all raised on fairy tales. A lonely maid puts on a glass slipper and meets her Prince Charming, a lonely little mermaid becomes a real girl and marries her Prince Charming, a lonely village girl gets abducted by a beast who turns out to be Prince Charming … in short, there are plenty of Prince Charmings to go around, especially if you happen to be a cartoon.

But what about real life? Sure, we'd all love to be abducted and held against our will by a big hairy beast; it beats having to get a college degree. But can real life become a fairy tale?

Is there any hope for you?

Well, let me tell you a little story.

There once was a little girl whose mother told her that no one would ever marry her. But this little girl thought that if she was intelligent, had a good sense of humor, and made a lot of money in her chosen field she would find a man to love her. And guess what?

This girl became an actress on a big hit TV show. She was beautiful, and charming, and somehow always very tan, and she made millions and millions of dollars.

And just when she thought life couldn't get any better …

She found a handsome, smart, talented man—her Prince Charming!—and they fell in love and lived happily ever after.

Just kidding!

The woman's Prince Charming met a woman named Angelina Jolie, and they ran off together.

That's right, that couple was Jennifer Aniston and Brad Pitt. Or Laura Dern and Billy Bob Thornton. Or Angelina's brother and whoever he was dating before Angelina started dating him.

The point is that this book will try to help you, but if you let your man anywhere near Angelina's perfect, man-sucking cooch, there is nothing I can do for you.

Before we go any further, I want to reassure the reader that I know it might be hard for her to trust my advice. After all, no matter how awesome I am, I am not famous. And we all know that whether it's Martha

Stewart telling us how to poach an egg or Dina Lohan telling us how to raise children, the best advice comes from famous people. That's why I'm starting many of these chapters with a letter written just for you, the reader, by a certified famous person.[1] And who better to start us off than the most famous man in daytime, Dr. Phil McGraw!

---

[1] Attention litigious celebrities: This is my confession that no celebrities wrote anything for this book. If you still wish to sue me, I am represented by myself pretending to be celebrity lawyer Gloria Allred.

Ladies, I Love You

A LETTER FROM DR. PHIL

Dear Ladies,

Oh, hello. Don't mind me, I always smoke my pipe by the fire with no shirt on. Does that make you uncomfortable? Good.

Sometimes in life, we need to feel uncomfortable in order to change.

But you know what's not uncomfortable? Baby oil. Why don't you grab that bottle I've left out on my leather settee?

Do you like leather? I do. Pleather, leather, vinyl, mesh, I like it all. My wife Robin has a very nice leather evening gown that I bought her for the Daytime Emmys.

Where's Robin, you say? Ooooh, she's just having a little "Special Cellar Time." It's important for couples to have separate activities. That's how we keep our marriage fresh.

You seem tense—why don't you have a little lie-down on that bear rug? Be careful. That bear is still alive. We became friends when he was a guest on my show during Bear Week.

Would you like some champagne? I drink mine from a bucket.

Well, I brought you here today to tell you that you are great. The only thing getting in the way of you having a great relationship is you! There are so many great things about you. Your hair is shiny, your eyes are pretty, your hands are great for grabbing. You keep your apartment very clean. How do I know that?

I've been living in your closet for six weeks. Don't worry. It's just part of my research for the show.

How have I survived in there? Lunchables and malt liquor. Don't scream. You'll wake the bear. I just want you to know that you are a beautiful woman who deserves to have happiness in your life. That's why I've decorated the attic as a replica of your childhood bedroom just for you.

Don't bother trying the door.

I promise that I am going to be there for you forever. As long as you don't try to scream or run. Or talk. Or hum. Humming really bugs me. The last girl hummed.

Remember, only you can make you happy, so if you are unhappy in the attic, it's because of you.

Now, please go to your room. *Entourage* is starting.

Love you,

Dr. Phil McGraw

Now that you've gotten that boost of confidence that only Dr. Phil can give, you're ready to jump into the dating pool. But please don't wear a bathing suit. Let's not be too confident!

GETTING STARTED

Now, in my original book, *I'm Perfect Just the Way I Am—Join Me!*, I advised women to "just be you," imperfections and all. I counseled women that the best way to meet men was to pursue hobbies and activities that they loved, so they could meet someone with common interests.

But after perusing some of the other literature available to help women with dating, I realized that there is only one way to figure out who your perfect mate might be.

That's right: a Dating Compatibility Quiz.

Once you've finished this quiz, you'll have a better idea of what you're looking for in a partner and why you're way, way too flawed to ever find it!

Please respond to the following statements with the number from this chart that is most appropriate:

1	Strongly disagree	6	Too drunk to answer
2	Somewhat disagree	7	Thought I strongly disagreed, but now I only somewhat disagree
3	None of your business	8	Sleepy
4	Ask again later	9	Signs point to yes
5	Agree strongly	10	Fuck you

PART I

ABOUT
YOU

___ I do things according to a plan.

___ A plan ... to take over the U.S. government.

___ With an army of super-intelligent robots.

___ I take time out for others.

___ And by "others," I mean aliens.
Space aliens. From space.

___ I love to help others.

___ Help them take over the government.

___ I seek adventure.

___ The kind of adventure that you have when amassing an army of space
aliens and super-intelligent robots to take over the U.S. government.

PART 2

SELF-
DESCRIPTIONS

Please use the numeric scale to denote how well each of the following words generally describes you:

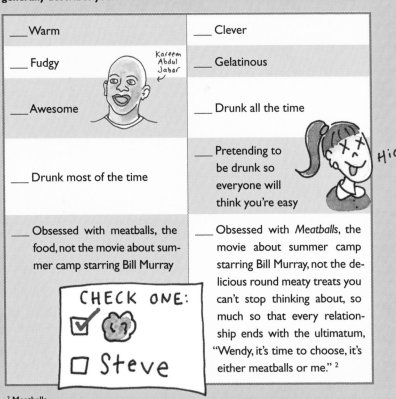

___ Warm

___ Fudgy

Kareem Abdul Jabar ↙

___ Awesome

___ Drunk most of the time

___ Obsessed with meatballs, the food, not the movie about summer camp starring Bill Murray

CHECK ONE:
☑ 🍝
☐ Steve

___ Clever

___ Gelatinous

___ Drunk all the time

___ Pretending to be drunk so everyone will think you're easy

Hic!

___ Obsessed with *Meatballs*, the movie about summer camp starring Bill Murray, not the delicious round meaty treats you can't stop thinking about, so much so that every relationship ends with the ultimatum, "Wendy, it's time to choose, it's either meatballs or me." [2]

[2] Meatballs.

Okay, now pretend that your friends have to choose just three of the words from the following list to describe you. Check the three items they would choose.

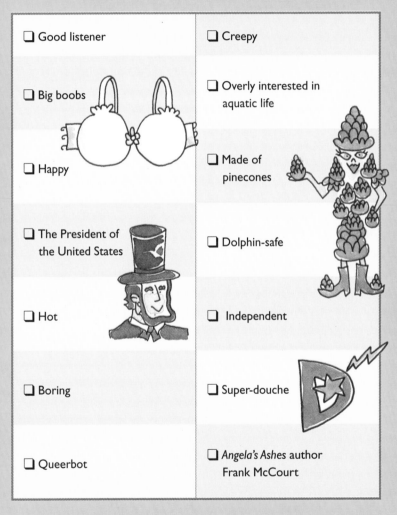

- ☐ Good listener
- ☐ Big boobs
- ☐ Happy
- ☐ The President of the United States
- ☐ Hot
- ☐ Boring
- ☐ Queerbot

- ☐ Creepy
- ☐ Overly interested in aquatic life
- ☐ Made of pinecones
- ☐ Dolphin-safe
- ☐ Independent
- ☐ Super-douche
- ☐ *Angela's Ashes* author Frank McCourt

PART 3

PERSONAL CHARACTERISTICS

Use the numeric scale to indicate how well each of the following describes you.

____ My friends come to me when they are in trouble because they know I can handle it. Also, I always have really good weed.

____ I get upset easily. Especially when I run out of weed. [3]

____ People who are controlling irritate me. Especially when they try to control my weed smoking. Fuck you, Dad. You'll never understand how awesome I am.

____ I think it is important to express my thoughts and feelings. Like have you ever thought how maybe what I call "blue" is the color that you call "red," but we'll never know because we can't get into each other's heads? I mean, that's like what life is like, right? We'll never know how another person sees the world. Man! My brain is working so good right now. Do you have any Cap'n Crunch? I could totally eat some fucking Cap'n Crunch right now.

____ I prefer not to be around people who have emotional swings. Like my mom. She's all, "Wendy, move out of the house. You're thirty-one." Shit. It's like nobody *gets it*.

[3] If this describes you, please call me immediately. I need to talk to you ... because I'm in trouble ... not because I want some of that weed. But, I mean if you really think about it, weed is really helpful when you are in trouble. Like if you were hiking and you got your arm caught under a rock, don't you think you'd be a lot calmer if you could smoke a joint with your other hand? Or say you were in the Donner Party and you were starving. It would be a lot easier to eat your friends and family if you were high. Believe me. Last summer I went to Yellowstone National Park with my family, and we forgot to bring a picnic on our two-hour hike. I would have found it a lot harder to eat my brother Ken if I hadn't been totally stoned.

___ I tend to either like someone a lot, or dislike him/her a lot. But you know who I fucking *love*? Oh shit, you know, that guy. That one guy ... I can't think of his name but I can, like, picture him. Red hair, he's like really funny. He's ... oh fuck it, I can't remember. Do we have any more weed?

___ I like to be pampered. No, I mean seriously. I love to poop my pants.

___ I generally feel better when I am around other people. As long as those people are not my parents. Riiiiiiiight?!? High five.

___ When I get mad I tend to take it out on someone. Like, I am so mad about the war in Iraq. Like I won't even watch the news because it makes me mad.

___ I try to understand the other person. Unless that person is the President, because that guy, man. I don't want to hear him talk. Like have your war and stuff but I am going to do everything I can to stop it. I am totally going to make a plan soon to do something about it.

PART 4
ABOUT YOUR
FEELINGS

Please write whether you experience the following feelings rarely, occasionally, or almost always.

1. Happiness _____

2. Sadness _____

3. Craving for Chicken Nuggets _____

PART 5

IMPORTANT QUALITIES

Please write important, somewhat important, or not important at all next to the following statements.

1. My partner's personal values _____

2. My partner's "Beyoncé-ness" _____

3. My partner's sex appeal _____

4. My partner's ability to look the other way when I am looking at pornography _____

5. My partner's ability to look the other way when I am starring in pornography _____

6. My partner's ability to look the other way when I am making him/her star in pornography _____

7. My partner's ability to ignore the fact that all of the pornography we are making and watching involves the Snorks _____

8. How much cake my partner can eat in one sitting _____

9. Whether my partner is alive _____

FILL-IN-THE-BLANK
Please write down the three most important things in your life. I've done mine below as an example.

1. Ham   1. _____

2. Cheese logs   2. _____

3. Cake   3. _____

PART 6

PERSONAL
BELIEFS

1. Which of the following gods do you worship?

❏ Christian	❏ Jewish
❏ Muslim	❏ Celebrities
❏ Baby Jesus	❏ Hindu
❏ Buddhist	❏ Self
❏ Odin	❏ Hot Yoga Teacher
❏ Talking Strawberry	❏ Christian Slater
❏ Baby Suri	❏ Dalai Lama
❏ Regular Llamas	❏ Pamela Anderson
❏ Louie Anderson	❏ Anderson Cooper

2. Which of the following groups would you like your partner to be involved in?

❏ Christianity	❏ Judaism
❏ San Francisco 49ers	❏ Black Sabbath

❏ National Organization for Women	❏ National Organization Against Women
❏ Current or Former Cast Member of *Law & Order*, up to and including Sam Waterston	❏ Fatties
❏ Gremlins	❏ Goonies
❏ Intellectuals	❏ Republicans
❏ Intellectual Republicans	❏ Kurds
❏ Muslims	❏ Pantywaists
❏ Scientologists	❏ Intellectual Pantywaists

PART 7

YOUR PERSONAL INTERESTS

Please use the numeric scale to rate your interests in the following things:

1. Underoos __   2. Unicorns __   3. Underoonicorns __

PART 8

GENERAL INFORMATION

1. Gender: ☐ Male ☐ Female ☐ Undecided

2. Age: ☐ Young ☐ Old

3. What age should your match be? ☐ 21 ☐ 22

4. What is your current marital status?
   ☐ Never Married
   ☐ Divorced
   ☐ Widowed
   ☐ Self-Widowed
   ☐ Crone

5. Would you like to start a new family by having or adopting a baby? ___

6. If yes, would it be OK if that "baby" was a thirty-one-year-old semiemployed writer with anxiety problems and twenty extra pounds? ___

7. Please write your address here, and describe your house, including whether or not my room would have a hot tub.

   _____
   _____
   _____

   _____
   _____

8. Choose the category that describes your highest level of education:

   ☐ Doctorate   ☐ Appeared on *The Bachelor*
   ☐ Master's   ☐ Some college
   ☐ Masters of the Universe   ☐ High school
   ☐ Bachelor   ☐ Did not complete high school

❑ Completed high school but bear terrible grudge against class-mates and am planning to kill all the popular kids at my high school reunion

9. Please write down your personal income_____

10. Please write down your Social Security number_____

11. Please write down the sixteen-digit account number on the front of any major credit cards, and the three-digit security code on the back

_____

12. Please write the following:
Mother's Maiden Name _____
First Pet's Name _____

13. Check one: ❑ Fatty ❑ Nonfatty

14. What is your ethnicity?

| ❑ White | ❑ Black | ❑ Hispanic |
| ❑ Asian | ❑ Arab, Terrorist | ❑ Arab, Nonterrorist |

15. Check one: ❑ Beautiful ❑ Not Beautiful

Scoring the Quiz

Congratulations! You've now finished my in-depth personality quiz. Let's score it using my scientific scoring method. Here's how to calculate: Look above this paragraph and see whether you checked the word "beautiful."

If you did, your personality type is **BEAUTIFUL.**

That's right, you are **BEAUTIFUL.**

BEAUTIFUL people should date: Anyone they want!

If you checked "Not Beautiful," your personality type is **NOT BEAUTIFUL.**

NOT BEAUTIFUL people should date: Anyone who will have them!

Great! Now that you truly know who you are and who is best for you, it's time to move on to some basic dating advice. Even before you go out on that first date, you need to make sure you have a strategy. That's why I've developed a foolproof plan for finding and keeping the man of your dreams.

SPARE THE R.O.D., DIE ALONE

When I started dating my husband, we were already friends, so instead of nerve-wracking formal dates, we just kind of hung out. While I thought at the time that this sort of low-pressure situation was good for us, I now realize it was boring and lame. I should have constantly demanded that he treat me like a princess and spend tons of money on me. Remember that the precedent you set while you are dating is how your hubby will treat you once you get that ring. Because of how our relationship started out, my husband and I haven't even been exciting or volatile enough to get divorced! It's shameful, but you don't have to make the same mistakes I did.

How can you avoid those errors? Well, let me introduce you to my friend R.O.D.

Who's R.O.D.? Well, he's not a person! R.O.D. stands for Rules of Dating.

By following these patented Rules of Dating, you'll find that the man you're involved with treats you exactly how you want to be treated from the first date right through to the traumatic divorce!

1 KEEP HIM WAITING.

If a man is going to date you, he needs to understand that the dating will happen at your pace. By keeping control from the very beginning, you let your date know you are in the driver's seat.

When a man appears at your door to take you on a date, you should ask him to wait in your living room while you finish getting ready. Then, leave your house through the back door and go see a movie by yourself. Any movie will do, but it's best if it's a really long one. After the movie, return to your house and tell your suitor you are ready to go. But, just as you are about to get in the car, claim that you forgot something, then run back inside and lock the door. If the man tries to enter the house to see what happened to you, call the police and have him arrested. Lastly, file a restraining order against him.

As we learned from Pamela Anderson and Tommy Lee, not being able to come within five hundred feet of you is going to make him want you all the more.

2 BE MYSTERIOUS!

Men don't want to ask women out if they already know everything about them. Your job is to give him a little bit of information at a time so he'll stay interested. For instance, if your date asks you where you went to college, be vague. Say, "At a place." If he asks you where you grew up, say, "Around." If he asks where you would like to go to dinner, grunt and gesture toward the sky.

3 NEVER PAY FOR A DATE, AND ALWAYS GET PAID FOR A DATE.

If a man wants to earn you, he's going to have to pay! Don't be a doormat when the check comes. Going dutch is the surest way to tell a man you don't value yourself. R.O.D. girls should always get paid for their time. Tell a man at the start of the date how much it will cost him—for instance, three hundred dollars for two hours or a thousand for the whole night. Then get the money up front. This is how men expect a classy woman to behave.

4 NEVER SLEEP WITH A MAN ON THE FIRST DATE.

We all look ugly when we're sleeping, so after you've let him do whatever he wants to you, get out of the car or leave the alleyway, and don't let him see you sleeping. In fact, try not to even have any lengthy blinks during the night because he might get disgusted and throw you away.

5 KEEP YOUR GUARD UP.

Don't be one of those girls who ends the first date by professing your love or asking when you'll see the guy again. Let him know that you are very busy and/or emotionally unavailable. For instance, try ending a date like this:

"Chad, I really enjoyed our date tonight, but I am shipping out tomorrow to fight the Germans. I know you don't understand this now, but I promise to try to write to you if I survive the Normandy invasion. Now get the hell out of here."

6 NEVER BE THE FIRST TO CALL AFTER A DATE.

No matter what happens, never, ever call a guy after your date. In order to show how important this rule is, let me tell you about my friend Lindsey. Lindsey went out on a date with a lawyer named Zachary. The next day, Lindsey was driving to work when her car was hit broadside by a bread truck and went tumbling down a cliff into a ravine. Lindsey was pinned into her seat by a tree branch, but as she landed in the ravine her phone fell out of her purse and the impact caused it to dial the number of the last incoming call—Zachary the lawyer.

Pinned into her seat, and on the verge of death, Lindsey heard Zachary answer the phone. Because she was following R.O.D., she didn't say anything. She didn't want Zachary to think she called him because she was desperate.

Zachary hung up the phone, and Lindsey died, but she died *with dignity*, and that is what R.O.D. is all about!

Finally, before you go out on that first date, you need to know how far you are willing to go with a guy. Luckily, the R.O.D. Putting-Out Spreadsheet makes that easy!

PUTTING OUT: THE SPREADSHEET

So, now that you've followed R.O.D. and snagged that eligible bachelor, it's the end of the night, and soon the awkward transition to physical contact will begin. It can be hard to know what's appropriate: A hug? A kiss? S&M play with a ball gag and a glass double-dong?

Rather than relying on your own personal morality, use this handy clip 'n' save spreadsheet. Just tally up how much your date spent on you and reward him appropriately.

AMOUNT	REWARD
$5-$10	Handshake
$10–$20	Warm hug
$20–$50	Awkward high five, segueing into a gentle cupping of the buttocks
$50–$100	Dry handjob
$100–$200	Greasy handjob
$200–$500	Free carwash
$500–$1,000	Blowjob or standard penetration
$1,000–$2,000	Butt sex
$2,000–$5,000	The lady will allow the gentleman to have sex with any number of her sisters or cousins
$5,000–$10,000	Three-way with guy dressed in giant pizza suit, up to three toppings to be selected by the gentleman

$10,000–$50,000	Spanking or light name-calling, poking in the buttocks with semisharp stick
$50,000–$100,000	Conversation, tea, rimjob
$100,000–$500,000	Three-way with guy dressed in giant pizza suit, up to five toppings to be selected by the gentleman
$500,000–$1,000,000	Confession of family secrets, exchange of favorite recipes, cunnilingus, spooning
$1,000,000–$2,000,000	Gentleman may choose either sex in bathroom of first-class section of 747 en route to Milan, Italy, or Xbox 360 game system with two free games
$2,000,000–$5,000,000	Pedicure
$5,000,001	Sexual intercourse with a female musical theater star of the gentleman's choosing
$5,000,002–$10,000,000	Manicure-pedicure with ball-cupping, giggling
Over $10,000,000	Three-way with guy dressed in giant pizza suit, up to ten toppings to be selected by the gentleman; French kiss

OK, now that we've taken the quiz, learned the rules, and memorized the spreadsheet, we're almost ready to move on to the advanced dating chapter.

But wait, before we go, let's take a quick look in the mirror.

I know, ick!

We can't go out looking like that. But a real physical transformation could take years, right?

Wrong! That's what I used to think, but by doing a lot of research, and by research I mean watching movies on HBO, I've realized that becoming a marriageable female hinges on only one thing: undergoing a ...

MAKEOVER MONTAGE!

There are many great movies about girls who go through life-changing makeover montages. Just figure out which of the following scenarios best matches you, then follow the plot of the story in your own life!

Scenario One: *Pretty Woman*

APPROPRIATE IF YOU ARE CURRENTLY: A prostitute.

This is the true story of a Hollywood prostitute who meets a rich man who transforms her. He doesn't mind that she's a prostitute, because once she's had a makeover, she's a classy, marriageable woman who just happens to be able to suppress the gag reflex.

The first step in the montage is to live in a run-down apartment in a cracky part of Los Angeles with Laura San Giacomo. Put on a pair of hot pants and hit the paves. Before you know it, a rich guy in a fancy car will pick you up and take you to a hotel in Beverly Hills.

The next day, he will give you his credit card and tell you to go on a montage, purchasing beautiful outfits from the 1980s.

If you choose the right outfits, you'll get to go to a lot of fancy events, that guy who played George on *Seinfeld* will try to rape you, and then your Prince Charming will realize that you are the woman of his dreams.

If not, he will send you back to the streets where you will eventually die of an overdose in an alley.

Either way, at least you got to have sex with that guy from *Sommersby*!

Scenario Two: *The Princess Diaries*

APPROPRIATE IF YOU ARE CURRENTLY: Secretly the teenage heiress to a fictional European throne.

This is the true story of a gawky-looking teenager with gigantic eyebrows who finds out from her grandmother, who used to be the governess in *The Sound of Music*, that she is going to be a queen. But you can't be royalty if you are unattractive, right? So a team of aliens get together and shave all of the teen's body hair off in a makeover montage. Or something. I didn't see the ending. But the movie made a lot of money, and that's what matters.

Scenario Three: *The Terminator*

APPROPRIATE IF YOU ARE CURRENTLY: A homicidal robot from the future.

This is the true story of a violent cyborg from the future who has trouble fitting in in the present. So, he steals the "cool" clothes of a biker. Then, he kills everybody and the world is destroyed in a nuclear holocaust.

Okay, now stage your own makeover by changing absolutely everything about yourself.

I'll wait while you do that.

OK, now that you are hot, it's only a matter of time before that previously unattainable hot guy (played by Luke Wilson) notices you (played by Anne Hathaway), and then he'll realize that his hot but bitchy girlfriend (played by Kelly Preston[4]) is no good for him. Next thing you know, your dad (played by Rutger Hauer) will be walking you down the aisle (played by Meshach Taylor) to the altar (played by Lisa Rinna and Harry Hamlin) and you're jetting away to your honeymoon in Hawaii (played by Vince Vaughn).

---

[4] John Travolta's pretend real-life wife.

In Conclusion

You've come a long way in just twenty-seven pages, and I bet you're almost feeling confident. Well, don't! We haven't even gotten you out there on an actual date, and believe me, the moment you feel confident and trusting is the moment that Angelina Jolie sneaks up behind you, hits you on the head, and whisks your date off to Ecuador to make love on a pile of orphans.

Yes, this scenario is extreme, but it happens every single day. And that's why before you start dating, you need to read the next chapter.

Sure, it would be great if there was some show called *The Bachelor* where single women could compete for the attention of a handsome, successful douche bag. But there isn't, so we have to get out there on our own and make it happen.

So turn the page, and let's get dating!

CHAPTER

CHECK

UP

LET'S CHECK IN WITH OURSELVES ABOUT HOW WE'RE DOING!

1. What did you learn from this chapter?

   _____

2. Really? Huh. That's not what I got from it, but OK, whatever I guess. Maybe try again.

   _____

3. Wow. That's an even crazier answer. Let's try something easier. Write down three changes you are going to make in your dating strategies based on my patented Rules of Dating system.

   _____

   _____

   _____

4. Do you really think that's going to help you?

   _____

Chapter 2

YOU'RE ALWAYS CHOOSING THE WRONG GUY

~ or ~

WHY YOU SHOULDN'T DATE GUYS WHO ARE TOO NICE TO DIVORCE YOU

~ or ~

IT'S NOT WHO'S JUST NOT THAT INTO YOU, IT'S WHO'S NOT JUST NOT THAT INTO YOU

PICKING THE RIGHT GUY

Before writing this book, I used to think that it was okay that I married a nice, good-looking guy who made a decent living and treated me with respect. But now I know that that is a losing attitude.

You are only going to get married six or seven times in your life, and you need to make sure each husband is someone you can really be proud of. He should definitely be famous, or at least famous in his field, and be either extremely handsome or incredibly rich.

Most importantly, though, he should not really love you as you are.

If someone accepts you, you will lose your motivation to constantly improve yourself. That is why even the most beautiful actresses marry losers who cheat on them, because they need to be reminded that if they slip up in any way, their asses will be on the curb. And in that spirit, it was obvious that when it came to this chapter's Letter of Inspiration, there was only one woman whose taste in men was impeccable enough to ask her to offer us advice about picking the right guys.

I Love Guyz Y'all!

A LETTUR FRUM BRITNEY SPEARS

Hey y'all. It's me,

Britney!!!

Spears, duh.

Furst of all, I just want to say thank you to all the fans. And to all of the haters out there, you just don't understand what it's like to be me. I have had to be rich & famous sense I was fifteen. It sux.

But, if there is one thing I've learned, it's that with the right man by your side there is no end to what you can accomplish!

In fact, I was married to the best guy in the world, Mr. Kevin Feder-line. Now, I know we are not together right now because I didn't work hard enough to stay hot. Did you know that when you are preganet, you get fat?

Well, you do! And then your man leaves you. But it's OKAY. Be-cause I'm a serviver, and I know I can get Kevin back. It's like that song "SexyBack" by Justin, only I'm bringing KevinBack. And how am I going to do it, by using my seven-step plan. It is awesome and easy to use because it only has six steps!

But before we get to that, I need to tell you my even better six-step plan for choosing an awesome man.

Here's the seven steps of it!

FINDING A HOT GUY

1. One way to tell if a guy is hot is does he have a girlfriend or wife? If so, he must be hot and you can date him.

2. Another way is is he a guy who can have kids? You can tell if he can because does he already have some?

3. You don't want a guy who is a pussy and afraid of you. If he can spend your money and not have a job, you know he is brave.

4. Can he dance?

5. Does his name rhyme with Bevin Bederline?

6. Also, can he not support you? It is good if he can't so you will stay motivated to make another album.

7. Do you love him so much it makes you actually crazy?

Okay, once you find a hot guy and you are together and then he leaves you, you need my seven-step plan for getting him back.

1. Have babies with him. Okay, y'all, you have to do this BE-FORE he leaves you, because babeez are kewt he'll want to come back and see them.

2. Get drunk. One good way to get somebody's attention is to drink too much. This makes people worry about you, and wooorying = attention = gettigback together.

3. Get rid of your hair. Hair freaks guys out because they are fraid they will get lost in it or it will smother them like some weird hair-monster. Shave it off.

4. Go to rehab. Rehab is awesum because everyone thinks you have changed, and then they will get back together with you.

5. Stage a comeback tour. Okay, y'all, you do not have to be famous to do this. You can dance ANYWHERE. If you live in a small town and your husband leaves you, just go down to the

mall, or even the mini-mall, and bring a boombox. Then, strip down to some cut-offs and a bra-top, turn on some tunes, and shake your butts! I bet you your man will come running back to you when he here's that you are dancing naked in the Dairy Qween parking lot.

Finally, and most importantly, you have to remind him why he loved you by showing everybody your naked lady parts as often as possible, and making sure that photographs of those parts are in newspapers and magazines. If you aren't famous like me, you can go down to the mall and get pictures of it taken at the GlamourShots store, then hang those photos up around your city for him to see.

Well, that about covers it. Remember, girls, we are smart, and we deserve to have the best guys out there, and then to be abandomed by them!

Love You,

Britney

Wow, that is one strong, brave woman, and I feel a little silly even writing more advice after that. But there are a few things that we can still learn about how to choose a man, as well as how to hold on to the one we've chosen.

Brit's advice was great, but she left out the most time-tested, foolproof method of mate selection, one that has been passed down from middle-school girl to middle-school girl since the beginning of time.

That's right, I'm talking about astrology.

ASTROLOGY: MORE FOOLPROOF THAN EVER

So, after using R.O.D. and the Dating Spreadsheet, things are probably getting hot and heavy with a certain special someone. But how do things look for the future?

We all know that the most foolproof way to analyze whether someone would be a good mate for us is to weigh the pros and cons of their likes, dislikes, and overall personality.

Kidding!

It's most important to get to know him based on his astrological sign!

The Aries Man

The Aries is also known as "The Ram." However, this does not mean that all rams are Aries. I made this mistake when I dated a ram, thinking we would be compatible. But it turned out the ram that I was dating was a Scorpio, and two Scorpios are definitely not compatible, especially if one of them lives in a barn and insists on staying with his flock even though you made *plans to have dinner with your parents!*

MOST COMPATIBLE WITH: Ewes.

LEAST COMPATIBLE WITH: Coyotes.

The Taurus Man

The Taurus is also known as "The Bull." He is stubborn and confident, and protects his woman. Again, do not try to date an actual bull. They aren't dangerous in romantic settings, but they tend to be boring, dividing their time between staring into space, eating grass, and bragging about their four stomachs.

MOST COMPATIBLE WITH: People who find guys with four stomachs *fascinating*.

LEAST COMPATIBLE WITH: Pisces.

The Gemini Man

Gemini is also known as "The Twins," and all guys who are Geminis have twin brothers. And as everybody knows, there is always a good twin and an evil twin. The evil twin will try to sabotage your relationship because he can't stand for his brother to have something he doesn't. Relationship will probably end with evil twin impersonating good twin, picking you up for a date, then driving you out to the desert and leaving you for dead.

MOST COMPATIBLE WITH: People who like having their abandoned carcasses feasted on by buzzards.

LEAST COMPATIBLE WITH: People who don't.

HOW TO TELL THE GOOD TWIN FROM THE EVIL TWIN

GOOD TWIN	BAD TWIN
Blonde hair	Gold tooth
Charming smile	Snarl
Job: pediatric oncologist	Job: kicking ass
Is named Chad or Brett	Is named Rock or Slade
No tattoos	Tattoos
Is a pussy	Is not a pussy

The Cancer Man

A guy with cancer.

MOST COMPATIBLE WITH: Julia Roberts in *Dying Young*.

LEAST COMPATIBLE WITH: Girls made out of asbestos or hexavalent chromium.

The Leo Man

Don't be fooled. This is Leo DiCaprio, movie star, gadabout, environmental warrior.

MOST COMPATIBLE WITH: Supermodels, tragic heroines aboard the RMS Titanic, Martin Scorsese.

LEAST COMPATIBLE WITH: Pesticides, Chevron.

The Virgo Man

Also known as "The Virgin," the Virgo male pledges at birth to remain a virgin for life.

MOST COMPATIBLE WITH: Nuns.

LEAST COMPATIBLE WITH: Sexually voracious nuns.

The Libra Man

Also known as "The Scales," the Libra is known for being a fair and balanced person. Unfortunately, all Libras have the power to weigh anything they hold in their arms, and any time your beloved hugs you, he will then be compelled to scream your weight out loud.

MOST COMPATIBLE WITH: People who like to have their weight screamed out loud.

LEAST COMPATIBLE WITH: Everyone.

The Scorpio Man

Do not be fooled! This is just a scorpion in a person suit!

MOST COMPATIBLE WITH: People to whom this sounds sexy:

"Mating starts with the male and female locating and identifying each other using a mixture of pheromones and vibrational communication.

The courtship starts with the male grasping the female's pedipalps with his own; the pair then performs a 'dance' called the 'promenade à deux.' In reality this is the male leading the female around searching for a suitable place to deposit his spermatophore. When he has identified a suitable location, he deposits the spermatophore and then guides the female over it. This allows the spermatophore to enter her genital opercula, which triggers release of the sperm, thus fertilizing the female. The mating process can take from one to twenty-five-plus hours and depends on the ability of the male to find a suitable place to deposit his spermatophore. If mating goes on for too long, the female may eventually break off the process.

Once the mating is complete, the male and female quickly separate. The male will generally retreat quickly, most likely to avoid being cannibalized by the female."[1]

LEAST COMPATIBLE WITH: See above.

The Sagittarius Man

The Sagittarius is "The Archer," which means he carries around a bow and arrow all the time, and is named "Robin Hood." He wears green tights and lives in Never-Never Land and can talk to animals.

MOST COMPATIBLE WITH: Woodland creatures.

LEAST COMPATIBLE WITH: People who embarrass easily.

The Capricorn Man

Is a unicorn!

MOST COMPATIBLE WITH: Rainbows, leprechauns, glitter-bombs, tears made of candy, magic.

LEAST COMPATIBLE WITH: Sadness.

The Aquarius Man

The Aquarius man is a water sign, which means that he is really into baths, showers, swimming in the ocean, ice cubes, and speaking to the dolphins in high-pitched dolphin-speak.

MOST COMPATIBLE WITH: Dolphins.

LEAST COMPATIBLE WITH: People with rabies.

---

[1] According to Wikipedia, so don't blame me if that's totally made up.

The Pisces Man

The Pisces man is a fish. He's a great companion for anyone who likes fish. He's delicious. But, if you're allergic to fish, having any contact with this guy will put you into anaphylactic shock. My husband is a Pisces, and I'm allergic to fish, and it's hard to deal with because we can never really be together. But we get past it by fighting all the time and sleeping with each other's friends!

MOST COMPATIBLE WITH: My friends.
LEAST COMPATIBLE WITH: Me.

CHOOSING AN ELIGIBLE BACHELOR

Now, I know you are looking at that last one, thinking, Wendy, shouldn't you feel comfortable and happy with your husband? Again, a reminder:

IF IT ISN'T HARD WORK, IT'S NOT WORTH HAVING!

Which brings me to my next topic—choosing an eligible bachelor to date. There are lots of unmarried guys out there looking for chicks, and plenty of married ones, too!

And if you are using my foolproof R.O.D. system, you're going to be pretending to be just the kind of independent, take-no-prisoners woman they're looking for.

But what should you be looking for in a guy?

The best kinds of men to date can be separated into four major groups. To make it easy on you, I've broken down the pros and cons of dating some of these catches.

Doctors

PROS: Doctors are natural caregivers who are intelligent and make a lot of money.

CONS: According to pornography, doctors are constantly surrounded by naughty nurses who need the doctors to "examine" them right away.

HOW TO TELL IF YOUR DOCTOR IS COMING ON TO YOU

There's no rule against dating your own doctor, though it can be tricky to tell if he's interested in you since getting naked with him is already part of the process, but here are a few signs that he may be coming on to you:

- He asks you to turn your head to the side and say, "I love you."
- He Photoshops his picture onto an x-ray of your heart.
- His lab coat says "Tight Butts Drive Me Nuts" on the back.
- When you lie down on the examination table, he insists on spooning.
- Before examining you, he washes his hands in Obsession by Calvin Klein.
- He tells you you have "sexy cancer."
- While giving you a Pap smear, he "finds" an engagement ring.

James Bond

PROS: Sexy super-spy with a license to kill.
CONS: Does not actually exist.

Family Members

PROS: These are people who know you and love you for just who you are. They are accessible because they often live in the same house.
CONS: Can't think of any.

Serial Killers

PROS: Usually single.
CONS: Will kill you.

POPULAR PICK-UP LINES USED BY SERIAL KILLERS

It can be tough to spot a serial killer because he won't just walk up to you and say, "Hi, I'm a serial killer."

But, by spending a lot of time at places where serial killers hang out,[2] I can tell you which pick-up lines they are using.

- Hey baby, you look so good in those jeans I'd like to chop your legs off.
- Was your daddy a thief? I'm not. I'm a serial killer.
- If I said you had a beautiful body would you stop screaming?
- That shirt looks great on you, but it would look even better in an evidence bag.
- Will you run away from me somewhere romantic?
- Do you come here often? I don't, because I only leave my underground cave when the voice of Marilu Henner inside my head tells me I have to find a new victim.
- I love you.

Any man from one of these four major groups will no doubt keep a girl happy and satisfied. Just imagine how impressed your mom will be when you show up at a family reunion with a hot doctor or famous serial killer on your arm.

Now, the savvier women out there will have already realized that I've left out one big category of eligible males, the holy grail of bachelors. Yes, I'm talking about …

MILLIONAIRES AND BILLIONAIRES

Obviously, there are lots of good reasons for trying to meet and marry a rich guy. They can take care of all your financial needs, and they are usually older and more mature than you are.

And since your husband is what I like to call your "grown-up Daddy," this makes rich guys perfect for the position.

[2] Applebee's.

C'MON LADIES, I'M NOT THAT BAD

By A. Wolf

Hi there, available females. I think you're great, and I'd love the chance to take you out for a meal or a movie, or even a Broadway play. I'm a thoughtful guy, and I really enjoy the theater, particularly the works of contemporary American playwrights Sam Shepard and Paula Vogel, though I'm also open to seeing that new *Legally Blonde* musical—I hear it's a fun romp.

I guess what I'm trying to say is that I'm more than just a wolf. I'm an interesting guy with a rich inner life. Sure, technically I'm a predator, but I'm a predator who really enjoyed *The Pilot's Wife* by Anita Shreve and cried during the last episode of *Six Feet Under*. I'm a docent at the Art Museum, a volunteer with Habitat for Humanity, and a multimillionaire (stock options from my time at Google).

I am always hearing how women feel that there are no eligible bachelors, no one who really understands them, and while that may be true of most human guys it is not true of me, Carl MacMillan, a wolf.

I'm not asking for a lifetime commitment, just a chance to prove to you that I'm a stand-up guy. I know I have a reputation for aggression, but as long as my ears aren't erect and my fur isn't bristling, I'm a pretty nice guy. But if you do want to have a future together, I make a great mate. And when it comes to having children, well, haven't you ever heard the term "raised by wolves"?

Sure, I may be a little rough around the edges, but I will treat you like a queen. I want to get to know you, build a relationship with you, and see where this thing can go. And I promise you that no matter what happens, there is no way I would ever eat you, baby. No way. Uh uh. Not a chance.

Unless you are delicious.

Surprisingly, I am not the first person who realized that millionaires are an attractive bunch. The information superhighways are littered with advice about how to meet and marry one of these hot little bachelor nuggets. I decided to get out there, try out some tips, and came up with my own little guide below!

HOW TO MARRY A MILLIONAIRE!

I. GO TO THE RIGHT PLACES. Millionaires are people just like us. They don't just go to fancy parties and elite restaurants. They like to go out for pizza or hamburgers, too. According to writer Marged Richards in her article on Handbag.com, the difference is, the pizza place will be in Bel-Air, and the hamburger stand will be in Saint-Tropez. So, in other words, you need to move to Saint-Tropez. If you are serious about meeting a millionaire, you have to do whatever it takes, even if it costs millions of dollars.

2. KNOW IT WHEN YOU SEE IT. If you aren't a super-rich douche bag yourself, it can be hard to spot one. But just remember this: A millionaire won't walk around wearing a gold-and-diamond crown, fingering a giant roll of hundred dollar bills and saying, "I am very, very rich. In fact, I am a millionaire." Rich people don't flaunt their wealth. But Marged Richards says the key is to look for a sign—like if the watch or bag he is carrying is something you've never even seen an imitation of, he's probably got lots of cash.

I followed my own advice on this one and it worked like a charm. Heeding the thought that I might find a millionaire at a pizzeria, I headed directly to the Saint-Tropez Pizza Hut. I sat down in a corner booth and ordered my usual, a large Meat Lover's Pizza, breadsticks, and the pan-seared halibut. Sure enough, after a few moments, I noticed a man sitting alone carrying something I've never even seen a fake version of: an endangered West Indian manatee.

They were sharing a Personal Pan Pizza and a twenty-piece Honey Barbecue Sauce Bone-Out WingStreet Wings.[3] I was so impressed by this millionaire and his endangered consort that I totally froze. What do you say to someone so out of your league? Well, that brings us to tip number three!

3. WORK ON YOUR APPROACH. Don't talk to millionaires about the stuff that interests you, like reality television or pie. Engage him in conversation about rich-people stuff. Try starting a conversation with one of the following prompts.

- Which do you think is better, the million-dollar bill or the billion-dollar bill?
- Do you slap your butler with the back of your hand, an open palm, or your calfskin gloves?
- Don't you agree that George W. Bush is an excellent king?
- Say, don't you think Mexicans are the best poor people?
- Wanna fuck?

4. FIND A SUITABLE DATING AGENCY. If you are having trouble meeting millionaires on your own, there are several matchmaking services set up to help you get to know rich bachelors. Some of the most popular are

---

[3] Available at select locations for a limited time.*

Millionaire Introductions, Discreet Connections, and, of course, 1-800-Chix-With-Dix.

5. DON'T TRY TOO HARD. Remember that rich people don't like to look slutty. Well, except for Paris Hilton. And Lindsay Lohan. And everyone else. You know what, forget it. Throw on a thong and a pair of animal ears, and go to the Four Seasons in Beverly Hills. Stand in the middle of the lobby bar and scream, "Free hummers for rich dudes!" What's the worst that could happen?

Great! Now that you've warmed up by dating a few millionaires, it's time to try some truly advanced dating by dating some billionaires.

DATING BILLIONAIRES

Billionaires are extremely sophisticated and intelligent, and you might have trouble keeping up with them in conversation. In researching this book, I myself went on dates with several famous American billionaires, and fortunately I taped some of our conversations so you will have some idea of what you are getting yourself into.

BILLIONAIRE ONE: DONALD TRUMP

ME:	Wow, Donald, this is a really nice restaurant.
DONALD TRUMP:	I'm amazing!
ME:	You know, I was reading today that they are developing computers that can actually transcribe musical recordings.
DONALD TRUMP:	You know who I like? Shakira. Have you seen the ass on that?
ME:	No.
DONALD TRUMP:	She's from Brazil.
ME:	Actually, she's Colombian.
DONALD TRUMP:	Don't ever contradict me. I'll slap you with my steak.

ME:	Please don't.
DONALD TRUMP:	It feels good! I used to hire a bunch of strippers to come to my house and beat the shit out of me with bone-in rib eyes.
ME:	That sounds made-up.
DONALD TRUMP:	I want to do some karaoke.
ME:	I don't think they have that here.
DONALD TRUMP:	Well, I didn't become an extremely impressive billionaire by letting people tell me when and where I can do karaoke.
	Sound of Donald standing, knocking over table.
OTHER DINERS:	Oh my God, run! He's going to steak-slap us!
DONALD TRUMP:	Waiter, I'd like to sing "I've Never Been to Me."
WAITER:	Right away, sir.
DONALD TRUMP:	And you, bring me a half-gallon of buttermilk and a baby pig.

BILLIONAIRE TWO: BILL GATES

BILL GATES:	You look lovely tonight. I hope you don't mind, but I brought you a present.
ME:	Wow, great, what is it?
BILL GATES:	A spaceship.
ME:	Like a shuttle?
BILL GATES:	No, it's a secret spaceship. I had it built specially. For the ladies.
ME:	Oh, I didn't know that.
BILL GATES:	You wouldn't. I had everybody involved with it killed.

ME:	Oh. Um, I have to go make a phone—
BILL GATES:	Sit down.
ME:	Okay. Um, why is no one else at this restaurant?
BILL GATES:	I had it built this morning, just for our date.
ME:	And you hired all these waiters?
BILL GATES:	Yes. Would you like me to have them killed?
ME:	No! Don't kill anyone. Please.
BILL GATES:	Let's go to the kitchen and select a baby deer to eat.
ME:	I think I'll just have the pasta.
BILL GATES:	Let's play chase and catch. Start running.
ME:	No thanks.
BILL GATES:	Wanna punch a lion in the face?
ME:	No.
	Long silence.
BILL GATES:	I just decided something.
ME:	You're having me killed?
BILL GATES:	Yup.

BILLIONAIRE THREE: OPRAH WINFREY

OPRAH WINFREY:	And now, joining me for dinner, WENDY MOLYNEUX.
ME:	Okay, please, I'm right here, you don't have to shout.
OPRAH WINFREY:	Look under your chair.
	Pause, I look under my chair.
ME:	There's nothing there.
OPRAH WINFREY:	Gotcha!

ME:	Okay, so I'm writing this book and I want to know what it would be like to date you.
OPRAH WINFREY:	Look under my chair.
ME:	I'm not going to fall for that again.
OPRAH WINFREY:	Come on. Just a peek.
ME:	Fine.

Pause, I look under her chair.

ME:	Oh my God, is that—?
OPRAH WINFREY:	Yep, I POOPED! [4]
ME:	I'm gonna go.
OPRAH WINFREY:	You get a car. You get a car. You get a car!
ME:	Oh my God. I do?!?!? Oh my GOD. I love you Oprah! I love you!

Well, I think that my billionaire dates were all rousing successes, and I wouldn't be surprised if you soon see a Page Six blind item asking, "Which slightly overweight unknown author was spotted canoodling with a billionaire in a secret spaceship just before she was thrill-killed?"

---

[4] Dear Oprah, Please don't get mad that I said you pooped. I know that you would never poop. In fact, you've probably evolved from the need to eliminate waste whatsoever, and now reprocess everything within your body as a kind of perfect, self-contained organism. It just seemed funny at the time. Please don't have me killed.

Sincerely,

Wendy Molyneux

INTERNET DATING

In the future, our dating problems will be solved by our personal love androids, programmed to service our every sexual need while having no emotions or needs of their own. (In the 1930s, 1940s, and 1950s these were called "wives.")

But since this isn't the future, you may want to try Internet dating.

Now even though I am married, I tested out some of the most popular online dating sites in order to help you decide which site best fits your needs.

I'll be coming to you throughout this chapter to let you know which ones helped!

MATCH.COM

According to Wikipedia—a notoriously unreliable online encyclopedia, and the only place I do research—Match.com is the largest online matching service in the world, boasting over 42 million members since 1995. They have offices in Dallas, London, Beijing, Tokyo, Munich, Stockholm, Madrid, Paris, and Boulder. This is great news for people who have a hard time dating in America because they are "different" or "a sex offender."

Like most sites, Match.com will ask you to fill out a profile and post some pictures of yourself. It's important to choose a few pictures that show different sides of yourself. For instance, when I signed up, I used these three photos of myself:

Match.com proved to be a reasonably good source for meeting guys. While I stopped short of actually dating these bachelors, I think these pictures seemed promising, especially that of "Tim" from Washington, D.C.:

I can tell he is a gentleman because he is wearing a tie.

eHARMONY

Unless you're dead (in which case, kudos to you for still reading; when I die, I'm just going to eat pie with Jesus and watch reality television), you've seen those awesome ads for eHarmony. You know the ones where some slightly overweight woman lies and says how great her relationship is with some gay-seeming dude? And it makes you want to never date again? Yeah, that one. You know how you always think there's something weird about that older doctor with the white hair and how he seems overly invested in your dating future?

Well, maybe you just can't accept the love of the Lord Jesus, who wants to save the world through stable heterosexual marriages. The white-haired guy in the ads is conservative Christian Dr. Neil Clark Warren, and he just wants you to be happy! As long as you aren't a total faggot.[5]

In his infinite wisdom, our Lord Dr. Neil Clark Warren has structured eHarmony so that if you are gay, you can't get matched on the site. That's right, you can't! You have to look for someone of the opposite sex. That's why all of the guys on the commercial seem kind of gay. They logged on hoping to find the man of their dreams, and then realized that if Dr. Neil Clark Warren doesn't want them to be queer, they should just find a lady!

So, how does eHarmony find your perfect marriage partner for you? Why, with a long, complicated personality test, of course! I took the test, and I found out that I am just as awesome as I expected, but I also found out that I am a lezzie, so by the time you read this, Dr. Neil Clark Warren will have had me killed.

ADULTFRIENDFINDER.COM

Now this is an awesome personals site. The best thing about it is that even if you are married, they are happy to help you find matches!

Right on the splash page, you can choose which of the following types of meaningful relationships you would like to have:

- ❏ One-on-one sex
- ❏ Group sex
- ❏ Discreet relationship
- ❏ Erotic chat/e-mail/phone fantasies
- ❏ Bondage and discipline
- ❏ Cross-dressing
- ❏ Miscellaneous fetishes
- ❏ Exhibitionism/voyeurism
- ❏ Sadism and masochism
- ❏ Other "alternative" activities

---

[5] In which case, he's really sorry: you're going to Hell.

Wowee! Right? I mean, finally, a site that really understands the kind of dating I want to do.

I was especially excited by the "other 'alternative' activities," because a lot of the shit I'm into isn't even listed on the splash page, such as:

- ❏ Duck play
- ❏ Advanced math
- ❏ Hot chocolate baths
- ❏ Mormonism
- ❏ Polite conversation
- ❏ Enthusiastic recriminations
- ❏ Chess-fucking
- ❏ Parking illegally
- ❏ Independent thinking
- ❏ Indigo Girls masturbation play
- ❏ Free admission to local theme parks
- ❏ Thai cooking

All in all, this was definitely the best dating site of all the ones I visited. Not that I really got to enjoy it. Once my stupid husband found out I was dating again, he got all "angry" and "divorcey" and I had to stop going on the sites, but I'll always remember you, Bigdixx69@earthlink.net. Thanks for the memories, and the butt sex.

In Conclusion

If with all the information provided in the preceding chapters you don't already have a ring on your finger, remember that it isn't my fault. It's probably because of your physical imperfections. So, just turn the page to my chapter on beauty and start getting your act together. Seriously, go. Ugh, I can't look at you one second longer!

LET'S CHECK IN WITH OURSELVES ABOUT HOW WE'RE DOING!

1. It's good to have goals. Let's set some. Which of these groups of eligible bachelors was most interesting to you? Let's make it a goal to meet one! Check all that apply:

   ❏ Doctors
   ❏ Millionaires
   ❏ Billionaires
   ❏ Serial Killers

2. Okay, now choose something more realistic.

   ❏ Serial Killers

Chapter 3

YOU LOOK TERRIBLE
~ *or* ~
PRETTY IS AS PRETTY LOOKS
~ *or* ~
IT'S NOT WHAT
YOU'RE EATING, IT'S THAT
YOU'RE EATING

LEARNING TO LOVE YOURSELF BY HATING YOURSELF

Before I started working on this book, I thought that the phrases "Beauty is only skin deep" and "Pretty is as pretty does" were just clichés, but know I know that they are lies. Dirty, dirty lies perpetrated by a media that's trying to get us to stop focusing on our looks and start focusing on developing our personalities. If I have to read one more story about Madeleine Albright, or how great 1997 Nobel Laureate Jody Williams is for her work on banning land mines internationally, I think I'm going to throw up on my prosthetic leg.

I wouldn't be helping you out if I let you believe that anyone is going to love you if you are carrying those few extra pounds, that weird hair color, and that faint hint of a mustache.

We all know that what makes a woman most beautiful is being super-skinny, having great hair, and being a total fucking bitch to everyone around her.

When it comes to feeling beautiful all the time, no one does it better than Tyra Banks. Not content to be just a stunning supermodel with a sweet, sweet A, Tyra Banks has created a media empire based on her *America's Next Top Model* franchise that has been syndicated around the world. Ms. Banks also hosts a daily talk show where she frequently addresses women's self-esteem issues as related to beauty. After pictures surfaced showing Banks looking a little pudgy, she went on her show in a bathing suit to show that she was not ashamed of her body. When she heard I was writing this book, Tyra begged me to let her write a letter of inspiration to my readers to help them believe in their own beauty. I agreed to let her do it if she gave me a million dollars. She said, how about I give her a million dollars instead? Because I don't really understand how negotiating works, I said yes.

Girl, You Look Fierce
A LETTER FROM TYRA BANKS

Hiiiiiiiiiiiiiii! First of all, let me just say that girl, you look fierce. Your ba-donk-a-donk is fierce. So fierce. And I am fierce. So terribly fierce. But. There was a time when I was young, when I wasn't so fierce. I knooooooooooooow. Hard to believe. I bet you thought I was a fierce baby. That I came out of the womb and was just fierce. Didn't you?

That question was rhetorical.

Rhetorical questions are still in the running towards becoming America's Next Top Literary Device!

Okay, where was I? Right. There was a time when I was not so fierce. I was a baby. A fat little baby who didn't even know how to pose.

Can you believe it?

You are a noted fashion photographer!

Anyway, I am here to tell you how I got through it. I used a little something called SELF-ESTEEM.

That's right, when I went around to modeling agencies when I was a baby, they would say stuff to me like, "You're a baby." And "Stop crying, baby." But I didn't listen to all that negativity. I just took it in, and it made me stronger. So strong. And fierce. A fierce, wild baby. I lived on raw steaks and the tears of other

babies. And before you knew it, I got discovered, and flown to France, where I crawled down the catwalk.
WITH DIGNITY.

So, what am I trying to tell you? I am telling you that you are fierce. But what is fierceness? Is it being a size 0? Is it?!? Is it?
Mister Jay!

Janice?

What's happening? I'm so cold.
LISTEN!

The thing is that you are the fierceness. So no matter what happens, remember that you are still in the running towards becoming America's Next Top Person With Self-Esteem. Can you be a model? Hell, no! Your thighs touch. But you can be anything you want to be. Including a model.

Look at me. Who would have thought that I could ever be a model? Well, everyone. Because of my hotness. BUT! What if I didn't want to be a fierce model? What if I wanted to be a fierce *doctor* or *policeman* or MODEL?

Well, I would have done it. Because I am still in the running toward being America's Next Top Anything I Want to Be. And so are you. Unless you want to be a model.
Work it!

I'm gonna go eat all my hair!

Love Always,

Tyra

So, now that Tyra's got us fired up, let's start by making a checklist of all of the things about you that are awful. Check off on the self-hatred inventory below which of the following problems apply to you.

HORRIBLE FLAWS CHECKLIST

❏ I am a fatty.

❏ I have "spider-lashes."

❏ I have problem skin.

❏ I have extra appendages or two or more heads.

❏ My hair is made of snakes because I am a Greek mythological figure.

❏ I am over twenty-five.

❏ I am smart, and it makes me ugly.

❏ I failed to start foot-binding at the recommended age.

❏ I wear glasses and am not Tina Fey.

❏ I eat one or more meals a day.

❏ I am OK with how I look (mental disease or defect).

Now that you've completed this self-inventory of your defects, you're probably feeling pretty disgusted with yourself.

And that's a good thing!

I used to think that it was bad to feel disgusting, but now I know that feeling disgusting is what motivates self-improvement.

So, let's start with the most common problem women claim to have— a few extra pounds.

But how will you know if you are, in fact, overweight?

Rather than messing around with some sort of complicated, lengthy, scientifically approved analysis of your height, weight, body fat, blah blah blah, just take the following dieting quiz.

DIETING QUIZ

True or false: I have an eating disorder.

If you answered "false" then you are definitely a fatty.

And what's the first step to losing weight? Well, it's getting F.E.D.

But wait, didn't I just say to stop eating? You bet! Because F.E.D. stands for Fashionable Eating Disorders.

FASHIONABLE EATING DISORDERS

I used to think that eating disorders were tragic and terrible, but then I noticed that many of the pictures of models in magazines looked just like pictures of girls with eating disorders.

So that must mean it's OK to have one, right? I don't know, maybe I'm not that smart, but I'm totally going to err on the side of caution by having one!

Below are a few AMAZING new ways to have an eating disorder, which you totally shouldn't do.

COMPULSIVE FOOD THROWING, OR CFT

The minute someone sets food down in front of you, immediately pick up the food and hurl it across the room. This will ensure both that you never eat your food and that people will think you are a celebrity. And that means one thing: lots of attention! And that's never bad.

HAMMER-HAND

You hire a "hammer-buddy." Every time you reach for food, he hammers your hand. Continue until your hands no longer work.

HIDE-Y FIND-Y

In this eating disorder, a team of specialists hides food around your house, and you can only eat what you find.

Then you throw it back up.

WIDE-EYED ORPHANS

For $12.95 per day, a squadron of adorable starving orphans will gather around your table while you eat, staring longingly at your food. We dare you to eat a single bite while these adorable, starving imps are around!

CANCER

According to the movies, there are ever-growing opportunities to get cancer, either by living in a low-income rural area near a power plant or by being the noblest character in a movie, preferably the beloved mother of a career-oriented child whose parent's cancer makes him realize that maybe there is more to life than being a hard-charging lawyer/journalist/hedge fund manager.

DIETS: THE FATTY'S ALTERNATIVE TO AN EATING DISORDER

Once you've chosen and executed one of these new-fangled eating disorders, get to work and don't stop until people are really, really worried about you! Remember that just because you are a size zero doesn't mean that your work is done.

I now personally wear a 3T—which is a toddler's size three! There's no better feeling than putting on a glamorous onesie for an evening out with my husband, and he loves that he can still fit me into a Baby Björn.

If you aren't mentally tough enough to handle an eating disorder, there are many popular diets out there that work for a lot of people. I tried all of the hottest plans so that I could recommend the very best one!

WEIGHT WATCHERS

This is a great program! After you sign up, you are assigned a "watcher," which is a supernatural being that follows you everywhere. This spectral being is usually pretty disgusting—just a heap of bones with giant, hypnotizing, googly eyes. Every time you take a bite of food, the "watcher" will let out a blood-curdling shriek. Trust me, after a while, you will not want to eat anymore.

With this program, you can choose either the "points" plan or the "core" plan. If you choose "points," you will be assigned to an NBA team and will be allowed to eat one calorie for each point you score during a regulation game. If you choose the "core" plan, you will be allowed to eat only apple cores.

SOUTH BEACH DIET

This diet was tough. You can only eat things that you'd find on South Beach in Miami, such as sand, sunscreen, and thongs. While it's OK at first, I got kind of burned out. Also horribly, horribly sick.

JENNY CRAIG

This diet is pretty fun. In order to be on this diet, you have to be a sitcom star from the 1980s who got really, really fat. The great thing is that you don't actually have to lose any weight on the diet. The publicists for Jenny Craig will just put you in slimming clothes so you can film commercials for their products. Then, when it becomes clear that you are a crazy disaster who wants to eat nothing but cake, tacos, and cake tacos, they'll let you out of your contract and sign up Valerie Bertinelli.

VOLUMETRICS

This was the diet declared by actual experts to be the most successful in helping people lose weight and keep it off. That's because it's based on the idea that people like to eat more rather than less. On this diet, you eat higher volumes of lower-calorie food. For instance, while I might normally have a chicken sandwich on white bread with mayonnaise for lunch, that contains things that are too calorie-dense—a whopping one hundred calories for a tablespoon of mayo!

Instead of the chicken sandwich, Volumetrics allows me:

> Three cups of tomatoes
> Two heads of iceberg lettuce
> One can of fat-free refried beans
> A large sheet of cardboard
> Two pounds of potatoes
> Twenty-two gallons of diet soda
> And for dessert, a moving box filled with sugar-free Jell-O gelatin

I really enjoyed this diet because I got to eat a lot, but I did find ordering in restaurants to be quite challenging, because they kept saying my orders were "crazy" and I needed to "get out" and they "don't serve food in moving boxes."

STARVING

While doctors might have declared Volumetrics to be the best diet out there, I think they may have overlooked starving. From the pioneers right through to modern-day Africa and Nicole Richie, we've all seen that starving can really work wonders when it comes to weight loss.

Starving isn't for everyone, however. For instance, people who like to eat or to be alive might have a hard time on this diet.

Now that you've pared off some extra pounds, it's time to start obsessing about something else, like fashion!

DRESSING FOR SUCCESS, OR AT LEAST TO HIDE YOUR OVERWHELMING SENSE OF FAILURE

Some people say it's what's inside that counts. Have you ever seen what's inside of you? Well, it's not a Prada bag or a cute pair of shoes, and it's actually pretty gross.

If you want to be a modern, successful woman, it's time to start dressing like one. Put on enough expensive clothing and people won't notice that inadequacy complex you're always carrying with you.

But if you have no sense of style, where should you start?

How about with ...

THE BASICS

When it comes to clothes, there are some basic things you'll want to consider.

FABRIC. It's best to wear high-quality natural fabrics like cotton, wool, silk, or endangered Giant Panda fur.

◀ To compare how artificial vs. natural fabrics look, here is a simple A-line dress in the artificial fabric polyester. Note how it clings to "problem areas."

And now here is the same dress in a natural fabric—beefsteak! See how the natural draping of the meats and the vibrant red color make the model look better? ▶

COLOR. Color is great because it helps you get attention. Just like that bright-orange cone on the side of the road, no one will be able to ignore you in the right color combination.

◀ See how this woman in her monochromatic grey outfit is yawn-inducing?

Here's the same woman in an eye-poppingly colorful outfit. I dare you to look away! ▶

PATTERNS. Patterns should be used sparingly, but effectively.

◀ Which do you prefer—this very plain black pantsuit worn with a white blouse?

Or this same pantsuit worn with a blouse with a dollar-sign pattern and a giant gold dollar-sign necklace? ▶
I thought so.

DETAILS. When it comes to clothing, it's the little details that count. Sure we can all wear a cute little dress, but why not add that special something that makes you stand out, like these:

BASICS YOU MUST BUY!

Here are the things you must buy as building blocks for your wardrobe:

BASIC BLACK PANTS. Everyone needs a good pair of black pants. However, since no one wants to make a baby with you, you probably have a lot of cats. Their fur will get all over the black pants. So, make sure you lint-roll your pants before you go out. Provided anyone has even asked you out. Weeping silently to yourself while you do this is optional.

A LITTLE BLACK DRESS. Every girl needs a little black dress. It's the most useful piece of clothing on Earth. You can:

Dress it up for an evening on the town!

Pair it with a blazer for work.

Use it to choke a ninja.

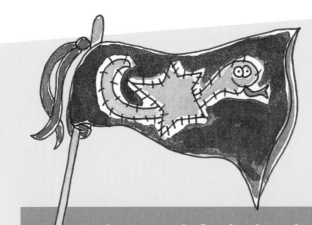

Fashion a crude flag for the independent nation-state you've created with your cats.

Use it as kindling to start a campfire if you get stranded in the woods.

Now, how little you want that dress to be is entirely up to you. Mine just covers my shoulders!

COWBOY BOOTS. Cowboy boots look great with anything from a pair of cute jeans to a sassy miniskirt and have been made into fashion staples in movies and by country recording artists. Remember that scene in *Urban* 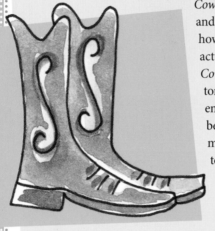 *Cowboy* when Debra Winger gets on that bull and rides it like a total slut? And remember how you only saw that movie because you actually thought you were renting *Midnight Cowboy* starring Oscar Award-winning actor Dustin Hoffman, but then you were too embarrassed to take it back and switch it because you go to the video store way too much and you feel like the clerks there are totally judging you, especially when you buy that king-size Junior Mints? And you just want to scream at them, "I'm not going to eat them all at once! You only sell one size! Besides, Junior Mints are a low-fat candy!"

EYE PATCH. Guys love pirates. Imagine showing up for a blind date wearing an eye patch and a parrot. Wouldn't that guy be surprised?!?

FAKE MUSTACHE. Every girl needs a fake mustache. Even in our modern era, sexism is still a factor in many work and social situations. If you find you are being discriminated against based on your gender, take out your fake mustache, stick it on, and watch that glass ceiling disintegrate.

Now, these basics work for almost anyone, but in purchasing the rest of your wardrobe you'll want to think about the bigger picture, your ...

BASIC BODY SHAPE

Using the handy illustrations below, find which body type matches you most closely, then follow the basic style guide accompanying each diagram.

SHAPE ONE: STRAIGHT

The straight shape is characterized by skinny legs, slim hips, minimal derriere, and an average bust.

IS THIS ME? If you're not sure if this is your shape, just ask yourself if you ever say this:

"I had such a hard time growing up, I was so tall and skinny that people thought I was a boy! I never had any confidence until a modeling scout approached me at a mall. Next thing I knew, I was flying to Paris for the runway shows. Then I started getting tons of work, and then after I booked that *Sports Illustrated* cover, I finally felt a lot better about the very light teasing I suffered as a child. (Pause.) Did I tell you that Sting is leaving his wife for me?"

WHAT SHOULD I WEAR? If this is you, you can basically wear anything you want! You can wear dresses, jeans, halter tops, shorts, tube tops, hot pants. A pair of panty hose with a glittery crotch and a bow tie? Go for it! A hat made of kittens? Why not! A suit of knight's armor and thigh-high boots? You bet. You won the genetic lottery, you beautiful bastard; now slap on a postal uniform, a candy necklace, some clogs, and a pair of chaps, and get out there!

SHAPE TWO: CURVY

The "curvy" shape is defined by wider hips, a bigger bust, and a knowledge deep down inside that when people say "curvy" they mean "kinda fat."

IS THIS ME? Well, are you kinda fat?

WHAT SHOULD I WEAR? You should wear something that plays up your assets. Like maybe in spite of being kinda fat, you're a nice person. So, wear a T-shirt that says, "I'm a nice person."

SHAPE THREE: PEAR-SHAPED

The pear shape is defined by being a pear—a giant talking pear with hands, feet, and big googly eyes.

IS THIS ME? If you have ever been told that people "don't like your kind" and you say "what kind?" and people say, "giant talking pears, asshole!", then this is you.

WHAT SHOULD I WEAR? Probably a tuxedo.

SHAPE FOUR: APPLE-SHAPED

The apple shape is just like the pear shape, only you're an apple. Also, it should be noted that unlike anthropomorphic pears, which are usually jolly, anthropomorphic apples are generally not very nice people and tend to be violent.

IS THIS ME? Answer this question: Am I a big, nasty apple?

WHAT SHOULD I WEAR? Um, whatever you guys want to. I think you always look great. Please don't hurt me, crazy, violent, anthropomorphic apple.

SHAPE FIVE: BOXY

The boxy shape is characterized by having six sides, with a top that opens and closes.

IS THIS ME? You may notice that people are constantly asking you to help them move, or saying things like, "Hey, you're a box."

WHAT SHOULD I WEAR? The bad news is that very little will look good *on* you, but lots and lots of

things will look good *in* you. In order to prove that to you, why don't you come by my apartment this weekend? I'm moving, and ...

SLIMMING FASHION TRICKS

No matter what your basic shape, everyone likes to dress to look slimmer. Believe it or not, a few slimming fashion tricks can help you look ten pounds thinner instantly.

TIP 1: DISTRACT FROM YOUR FLAWS

We all have body parts we don't care for. I, for example, have a hook for a hand and one giant eye in the middle of my forehead.

But the last thing you want to do is draw attention to your pudgier parts. If, for instance, you don't like the way your hips fill out your jeans, try to draw the eye upward by wearing a beautiful crystal vase on your head. Pair it with a mask of disgraced former President Richard Nixon, and I guarantee you no one will notice your hips.

TIP 2: USE PATTERNS TO YOUR ADVANTAGE

Patterns can be your best friend or your worst enemy. One time I made the mistake of wearing a bathing suit covered in swastikas to the beach. In that pattern, I felt gigantic! It would have been much more flattering if I'd worn a simple black bathing suit and a swastika armband.

Instead of wearing checkered pants and a T-shirt with a burning-cross pattern, why not try a monochromatic white sheet and hood? That will give you a longer, leaner look and is refreshing for the spring and summer months.

TIP 3: ACCESSORIZE APPROPRIATELY

The size of your accessories makes a difference. If you are tiny, carry a medium-sized purse that won't dwarf you. Conversely, if you are a plus-size, carrying an oversized purse can make you look a little smaller.

Remember that the hottest accessories right now are dogs and babies! The same rules apply here. If you are slim like Paris Hilton, go ahead and carry a little dog. But, if you are a bigger girl, carry a mastiff or German shepherd, and instead of having a baby, put a chubby fifth grader in your Snugli. Then sit back an wait for the compliments!

TIP 4: TAN, TAN, TAN

A great, overall tan will make you look instantly slimmer. There are a lot of great self-tanners out there, but I myself just go for a thick coat of butterscotch frosting. If all else fails, you can try being a black person. There are other advantages to this approach, such as being friends with Oprah and having cuter babies, though apparently some people still get treated badly because they are black. I have never seen this firsthand, because no black people have chosen to go to my schools or live in my neighborhood.

It used to be that people only expected you to be tan in summer, but with all the tanning options available now, a year-round tan is de rigueur. Worried about staying bronze through the winter months? Try one of these options:

HOME SELF-TANNERS

There are a variety of self-tanning creams and lotions you can use in the privacy of your own home. You may want to have help getting the hard-to-reach places like your back. I love tanning at home, and I captured and trained a wild stallion to help me get the self-tanner onto my back. I don't see any way in which that could go wrong.

TANNING BEDS

Tanning beds are very convenient and help you avoid the orangey look that is so common with self-tanners. Another advantage is that lying down in them is great practice for lying in your coffin at your funeral after you die of skin cancer.

SELF-TANNING BOOTH

This is a tiny booth that you go into and shut the door, and then a vapor shoots out at you from a wall. There are a few tips that will help you enjoy the experience:

- Wear protective goggles to keep product out of your eyes.

- Exfoliate and moisturize before your tanning session.

- Don't bring your senior citizen buddy Inga, the Holocaust survivor.

MYSTIC TAN

The Mystic Tan is a special supernatural tan that is induced through a séance. A medium comes to your home to call down the spirits of very tan people throughout history, such as George Hamilton, Anna Nicole Smith, and Pocahontas. George Hamilton isn't dead, but he still shows up, because what else is he doing?

DRESSING FOR YOUR "SEASON"

Now that we've established your basic body shape, in order to select which colors are going to look best on you, you'll need to determine which "season" you are. A lot of people erroneously believe that your "season" is based on your skin tone and hair color. In fact, your season is based on numerous other criteria.

Examine the checklist for each season. For each characteristic that describes you, give yourself a point. Whichever season you have the most points for will tell you your best color scheme.

SUMMER

❏ I enjoy outdoor activities.

❏ I am refreshing.

❏ I am a generally happy person.

❏ I enjoy the song "Summertime" from the musical *Porgy and Bess*.

❏ I enjoy the hit song "Summertime" by DJ Jazzy Jeff & the Fresh Prince.

❏ I think the DJ Jazzy Jeff "Summertime" is much better than the *Porgy and Bess* "Summertime," and I'm not embarrassed about that.

❏ I also think that "Parents Just Don't Understand" is a really great rap song.

❏ Whenever I am dancing, I claim to be "Gettin' Jiggy."

❏ I am a tool.

IF THIS IS YOU: You are a summer! This means that you are kind of a loser with terrible taste in music.

YOUR BEST COLORS: A T-shirt with a pretend tie on it. Those roller skate shoes even though you're forty.

WINTER

☐ I like being indoors.

☐ I enjoy being cozy.

☐ I like hot cocoa.

☐ In fact, I like being indoors so much that I never want to go outside.

☐ Ever.

☐ Because it's scary out there.

☐ Anything could happen.

☐ I could just be walking down the sidewalk and a car could come up on the sidewalk and hit me. Or if I drive my car, someone could come running out into the street out of nowhere, and what if I hit him without seeing him, and then I'd have to drive around and around the block to verify that I didn't hit anyone? Plus, one in four people will get skin cancer in their lifetime. What if a bird pecked my eyes out? Or a crazy raccoon attached itself to my throat? What if some of that space junk landed on me? I'm so cold. Hold me. So cold.

IF THIS IS YOU: You are a winter. You're also crazy!

YOUR BEST COLORS: A bomb shelter that you dig in the backyard.

FOOTBALL

☐ I am boring and overrated.

IF THIS IS YOU: You are a football season. Which means that you are interminable and awful and everyone loves you but me.

YOUR BEST COLORS: Go away.

IF THIS IS YOU: You are a hurricane season! Even though people know you're coming, they fail to adequately prepare for you, and sometimes after you've gone, you help everybody achieve high levels of racism.

YOUR BEST COLORS: White people.

PLASTIC SURGERY: A SUBTLE WAY TO TELL THE BABY JESUS HE MADE YOU WRONG

So, now you know your basic body shape and have purchased a basic wardrobe, become shockingly thin, and figured out your "season." Wow! You must be perfect, right?

No. No, no, no. How many times do I have to tell you that your work is never done?

Do you think that perfect-looking Hollywood starlets look in the mirror and think, "I'm okay?"

No, they look in the mirror and think, "What surgery do I need next?" And that's what you should be thinking, too.

Sure, surgery can be scary, and the side effects can spook you.

In fact, you could actually die. But, if you aren't pretty, aren't you kind of dead already?

Even if you are a perfect size double zero with fantastic hair and great skin, you can't stop the march of time. Yes, no one can evade the withering effects of age, adding extra pounds and wrinkles to even the most perfect woman.

If only there were some sort of medical procedure that could help us ladies retain our youth and good looks, alas … Wait, what's that you say? Plastic surgery? Well, what is this … miracle that can help us look like we're in our twenties well into our forties, fifties, sixties, and beyond? What's that you say? You don't believe me? You say this miracle can't possibly be real?

Well, negative nellies, if you need proof look no further than this:

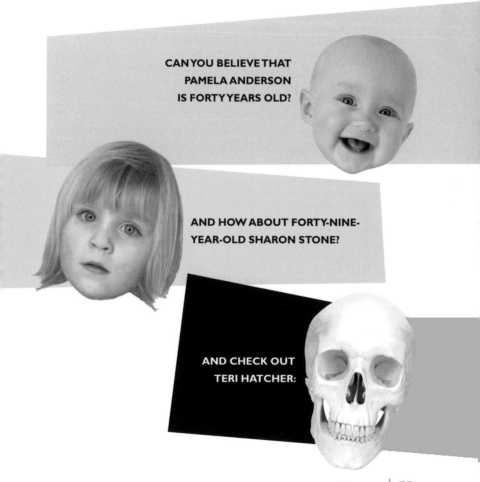

CAN YOU BELIEVE THAT PAMELA ANDERSON IS FORTY YEARS OLD?

AND HOW ABOUT FORTY-NINE-YEAR-OLD SHARON STONE?

AND CHECK OUT TERI HATCHER:

So, now that you've decided to get plastic surgery, you have a lot of great options. Here are some of the most popular, cutting-edge treatments available.

NOSE JOBS

This is one of the most popular kinds of plastic surgery. Also known as rhinoplasty, the procedure involves reshaping the skin and cartilage to give the patient a prettier or more youthful appearance.

Recommended for:

- Anyone self-conscious about the appearance of her nose.
- Jews.[1]

BREAST AUGMENTATION

This is another very popular procedure. A woman may choose to have larger breasts either to boost her self-confidence or so her husband won't leave her. Technically known as "getting tig ol' bitties," more and more women are doing this every year.

There are several types of implants available. A patient may choose from the following:

- **SALINE BREAST IMPLANTS** are made of a silicone rubber sack filled with a saline solution.

- **SILICONE BREAST IMPLANTS** can be used instead. Silicone gel-filled implants are only offered on a limited basis, under approved studies, due to questions about silicone implants correlating to autoimmune diseases.

---

[1] This joke was approved by Jewish person David Iserson. He can be contacted with objections, criticisms, or information about how to save money on consumer products at davidiserson@gmail.com.

- **ZOMBIE BOOBS** are boobs stolen from a corpse and then attached to your body by a mad scientist. This can be awesome because they are real boobs, but if you accidentally get the boobs of a serial killer, they may develop a mind of their own and go on a killing spree.

EYE LIFT

One of the first places a woman might start to look older is around her eyes. The eye lift is an expensive procedure, but well worth it. Depending on how much you want to spend, you can have your eyes lifted onto the middle of your forehead or all the way to the top of your head. It's like having a sunroof for your brain!

BOTOX

Botox is an injection of the botulinum toxin, which can totally fuck you up if you happen to eat it, but when injected it only totally fucks up your face.

EXTRA HEAD

This procedure is a little less popular, but it's exactly what it sounds like.

TOTAL BODY REPLACEMENT

Many women these days are choosing total body replacement. As I said in the introduction to this book, there's so much wrong with us that short of becoming a totally new person, I'm not sure there's a lot of hope. But for the reasonable price of just one million dollars, your brain can be transplanted into the body of a hot supermodel, and then all of your troubles will be over.

In Conclusion

Whether you're starving yourself perfectly thin or freaking out about whether peep-toe shoes are still in, there's no doubt you're feeling better and worse about yourself than ever!

Should you really be expending this much energy trying to wrest your body into a shape you can never possibly maintain?

Well, just imagine having the happy, carefree, perfect life of Janice Dickinson or Gia or Naomi Campbell. Can all that happiness and joy be yours? Yes, yes it can.

And so I'm urging you to just forgo the rest of the advice in this chapter and schedule your full body replacement today. The future is waiting. Don't waste another minute being you.

LET'S CHECK IN WITH OURSELVES ABOUT HOW WE'RE DOING!

1. Remember how I wrote about Madeleine Albright at the beginning of the chapter? Do you know who that is?

   _____

   Me neither!

2. Do you look better or worse than you did at the beginning of this chapter?

   _____

3. Please use the rest of the blank space to list all of your remaining flaws. You may use extra scratch paper to complete this section.

   _____

   _____

   _____

   _____

   _____

   _____

   _____

   _____

   _____

Chapter 4

YOU'RE NOT VERY SMART

~ or ~

HOW MANY WOMEN'S BRAINS CAN FIT IN ONE MAN'S BRAIN?

~ or ~

IT'S NOT WHAT YOU'RE NOT LEARNING, IT'S WHAT'S NOT LEARNING YOU

I'll admit that before I started working on this book, I thought the idea that women aren't as smart as men had gone the way of the bustle (whatever that is!), but then I realized that if women were as smart as men, we'd definitely get paid as much as them for the same jobs. But we don't, and I think that speaks for itself. Or something.

All you have to do is read a little bit of history (if you know how to read) to understand that men are responsible for most of the significant contributions to science, religion, politics, and the performing arts. Men have come up with many of our most important and life-changing inventions, such as the printing press, the cotton gin, open-heart surgery, and the Holocaust!

In fact, just like it would take 93 million Earths to make up one sun, it would take 93 million women's brains to fit inside one man's brain. The female brain is so small it is actually invisible to the human eye. Is that really true? No. I made it up because I'm not smart enough to really know how big the female brain is. Plus, *Ugly Betty* is going to be on soon and I really need to finish writing this book by then! I wonder what hijinks Betty and her pals are going to be up to this week! OMG!

Anyhow, it would obviously be too much to ask for me to actually make you smart. I mean, I'm not a brain surgeon! But it is feasible that you can pretend to be smart. Why should you do this, you're wondering. Didn't you just spend three chapters telling us that it's what on the *outside* that counts?!?

Well, let me tell you a true story about a girl I used to work with. Let's call her Daphne. Daphne and I worked together in an office all by ourselves. Daphne had been dating a guy named Brad that I thought was kind of douchey. So, imagine my relief when Daphne told me that she and Brad were going to break up! Why? I asked. What happened? Well, it turned out that Daphne had read Brad's journal, in which Brad had written the following: "I don't think I can marry Daphne because she's not smart enough to be the mother of my children."

Wow, I said, good choice to break up with that guy! And then I proceeded to tell Daphne what a douche I thought Brad was, enumerating my every objection. Well, guess what happened?

That's right! Daphne got back together with Brad the very next day! And when I said, oh, sorry about all that stuff I said, but you can't really hold it against me, she made it clear that she was going to totally hold it against me! And then Brad broke up with her because she wasn't smart enough to be the mother of his children.

So what is the moral of the story? The moral of the story is that clearly Brad was right about Daphne not being very smart, and he would have been insane to let her mother his children! But you don't have to suffer Daphne's fate. After reading this chapter, you'll know how to pretend to be smart enough to have somebody's baby! But not enough to make you ugly!

When working on pretending to be smart, it's good to remember that you don't need to know a lot about one thing, but rather a little about a lot of things. This is what's known as being a *dilettante*. I don't know what that is, but it sounds like *debutante* so it must be pretty good.

And who knows more about pretending to be smart than the forty-third President of the United States, George W. Bush?

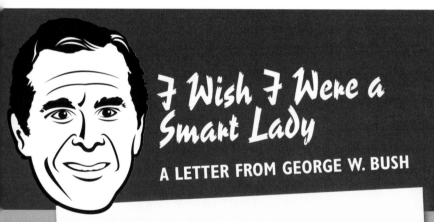

I Wish I Were a Smart Lady

A LETTER FROM GEORGE W. BUSH

Dear Women,

You know, a lot of people didn't think I was too smart before I became President of the United States, and I know a lot of people might think that ladies aren't too smart either. But that's not true. Just look at all the ladies in my life: my wife Laura, my girl-friend Condoleezza Rice, and one of my daughters. You know, the one that's not as pretty.

I always thought it would be nice to be a smart lady. Because then you could know all that secret mysterious stuff about periods and sewing and why you guys are always crying. Also, if I was a gal, I bet my Daddy woulda left me alone and not made me go to Yale and stuff. Yale was hard.

I always thought it would be nice to get to just eat candy and ride horsies and do that kinda lady stuff. I didn't want to go to war. It's just that they came to talk to me about it while I was in the middle of watching *Divine Secrets of the Ya-Ya Sisterhood*, and I signed some papers so they'd let me get back to watching it. I love Sandra Bullock. My favorite Sandra Bullock movie is probably *Miss Congeniality*, because I like beauty pageants and guns.

Sandra Bullock is a good example of being a smart lady. She has been in many blockbuster films, but she's also a down-home Texas gal, and her husband is that guy that makes trucks or jeeps or something.

I believe that women can be just as smart as men and can do anything they want to do with their lives. I mean, my own wife is a real iconoclast—a housewife and a librarian. Who ever heard of a lady librarian? Not me!

What's next, a lady home ec teacher or a lady nurse?

So ladies, keep reaching for the stars. Because this is America, which in Indian talk means "Land of the Lady." And maybe some day we could even have a lady president, or at least a lady president's wife.

Yours Sincerely,

George W. Bush

That was well put, and truly inspirational.

FEMALE ROLE MODELS

Sometimes, we all need a role model to look up to and emulate, especially when it comes to being smart.

But are there women out there who are smart and not disgusting? Well, sure. Let's take a look through history at some ...

HILLARY CLINTON

WHY SHE'S SMART: Quickly becoming one of the most important female political figures in American history, Mrs. Clinton has proven that you're never too successful to look the other way when your husband lets a chick half your age suck his dick in your house.

HELEN KELLER

WHY SHE'S SMART: Helen Keller was an ordinary girl until an illness left her blind, deaf, and dumb. She went on to earn fame for overcoming her handicaps, and she's an inspiration to all of the other blind, deaf, and dumb women in the world. Helen is also a cautionary tale. After becoming famous, she was known for her lavish lifestyle and diva-like demands, including that no one look her in the eye or address her directly.

MARY, MOTHER OF JESUS

WHY SHE'S SMART: Instead of having a regular baby, she had a Jesus baby. This move made her one of the most famous women in all of human history. But, you're wondering, isn't there just the tiniest chance that she just got regular pregnant and then pretended a magical angel made her pregnant? In which case, I reply, given what came after, doesn't that make her one of the *greatest geniuses of all time*?

BLAIR FROM *THE FACTS OF LIFE*

WHY SHE'S SMART: In the episode "Dope," even though she makes the mistake of trying marijuana once, she swears off of it when she sees that the paper she wrote on *Moby-Dick* while high wasn't very good at all. And the woman who played Blair is pretty smart, too! In fact, she wrote a whole book all by herself, whereas I've had my butler write most of mine. Her book is called *Creative Correction*, and it teaches you how to discipline your kids from a Biblical perspective.[1] I loved the part about when it's appropriate to stone your daughters and how many days locked up in their tomb your sons should spend if they draw on the walls.

FEMALE DINOSAURS

WHY THEY WERE SMART: Even though they're extinct, they got parts in the blockbuster hit movie *Jurassic Park*.

So see, there were a few smart ladies in the past and hopefully, with the help of brain transplant technology, in the future! Now that we're inspired by some of our smartest ancestors, let's get learnin'!

Let's begin at the very beginning … with some history!

[1] Seriously.

SHAKESPEARE
IS BORN

RENAISSANCE
TIMES

DARK AGES

JESUS

DINOSAURS

KNIGHTS,
PRINCESSES

UNICORNS AND DRAGONS
BECOME EXTINCT

FAIRIES AND ELVES
BECOME EXTINCT

BLACK PLAGUE

Now
what?

VIETNAM WAR ENDS

WOODSTOCK

WE PRETEND TO
GO TO MOON

JFK IS HANDSOMEST,
THEN DEADEST
PRESIDENT

I will never
regret doing all
this cocaine.

COCAINE IS
INVENTED

KURT COBAIN
DIES

BILL CLINTON
IS AWESOME

FUCK.

END OF CIVILIZATION
SIGNALED BY
ELECTION OF GEORGE
W. BUSH

WE FORGET TO
REMEMBER THE FIRST
9-11, AND THEREBY
DO NOT PREVENT IT
FROM HAPPENING

A Timeline of All of the History You Need To Know

Clip this timeline and keep it in your purse as a handy reference.

Now this is just a brief overview of history, just the bare bones. But what makes human civilization really interesting is the many cultural achievements along the way.

In the types of circles where you'll find the sort of rich, smart men you want to marry, you'll be expected to be familiar with certain books and works of art. Now, that doesn't mean you have to read all of those books. All you'll need to know is the basic story of each one, and then something insightful to say about it.

THE ADVENTURES OF HUCKLEBERRY FINN by Mark Twain

Huck and the runaway slave, Jim, set out on the adventure of a lifetime in this follow-up to *The Adventures of Tom Sawyer*.

SOMETHING INSIGHTFUL TO SAY ABOUT IT: Did you guys know that Huckleberry Finn was a person, not a berry? Also, I think that in almost all cases slavery is wrong!

CATCH-22 by Joseph Heller

I didn't read this one, but I'm pretty sure it's a book about baseball. I think it's a book about a sexy catcher who, even though he's just twenty-two years old, becomes an international superstar and dates a bunch of hot models.

SOMETHING INSIGHTFUL TO SAY ABOUT IT: Don't you think it's confusing that if the catcher drops the ball after a strike in baseball that the batter can still run? Also, don't you think that the funniest guy in baseball is Kansas City Royals player Mike Sweeney? Say his name fast and you'll see what I'm talking about.

THE CATCHER IN THE RYE by J.D. Salinger

This is a sequel to *Catch-22*, but written by a different author, just like how after V.C. Andrews died somebody kept writing books under her name. In this sequel, the hot catcher from *Catch-22* has to quit baseball because of a rotator cuff injury, and then he opens a deli on the Lower East Side.

SOMETHING INSIGHTFUL TO SAY ABOUT IT: Did you know that the popular deli meat pastrami is made from beef, and it's not some kind of weird ham? And sure it's embarrassing that you didn't know that until you were thirty-one, but there weren't any delis in suburban Indianapolis, were there?! No. Maybe I don't know what pastrami is, but I sure can tell you where you can get soup, salad, and unlimited breadsticks. It rhymes with Schmolive Schmarden, and it's delicious.

CRIME AND PUNISHMENT by Fyodor Dostoevsky

This is a Russian novel about something. I think it's about crime. And also punishment. The main character is named Raskolnikov, which means "rascal" in Russian. He gets up to all kinds of hijinks for which he receives a variety of punishments. Kind of like *Home Alone* with communists, I think. Or else it's about something else. I don't read Russian books because I am not a communist.

SOMETHING INTERESTING TO SAY ABOUT IT: In the pages preceding Raskolnikov's terrible act against his landlady, Dostoevsky characterizes his protagonist as suffering from a "sickness." While this sickness could be viewed literally (he is suffering a fever), I would posit that Dostoevsky's concept of sickness is a moral one, the sickness all humans carry that is nothing short of original sin. And only by passing through this sickness and coming to a state of personal responsibility can Raskolnikov, and therefore all men, be redeemed. Or whatever.

DON QUIXOTE by Miguel de Cervantes

I'm pretty sure it's about a donkey.

SOMETHING INSIGHTFUL TO SAY ABOUT IT: Don't you think it's weird that "donkey" and "monkey" are spelled almost the same but aren't similar animals at all?

GONE WITH THE WIND by Margaret Mitchell

An epic romance set against the backdrop of the Civil War.

SOMETHING INSIGHTFUL TO SAY ABOUT IT: Everybody likes to think that this is an epic romance, and that's why they like it … but don't you kind of think that people who really like it are kinda secretly racist? I'm just sayin'.

THE GRAPES OF WRATH by John Steinbeck

This is a great story about a family of angry grapes that has to move west during the Great Depression.

SOMETHING INSIGHTFUL TO SAY ABOUT IT: Do you think that the fact that I really wanted to write "the Grape Depression" means that I have lost my mind?

THE FIRM by John Grisham

Now this is an awesome book! It stars Tom Cruise as a good-hearted lawyer recruited into a corrupt law firm. Soon he finds that it's not only his career that's in jeopardy, it's his life!

SOMETHING INSIGHTFUL TO SAY ABOUT IT: Do you think that Tom Cruise is gay, or just strange?

I don't know the answer to that one, but maybe since he's a Scientologist[2] we'll figure it out after we've read our next section on science!

SCIENCE

It's a scientific fact that I got from some science that I made up that 99 percent of men like to talk about science on a first date. Why, the minute you walk down the stairs and into the arms of your waiting beau, he's likely to already be rattling on about space-age polymers, carburetors, or President Kennedy's space program. While you don't need to know how to split the atom (hint: butter knife), having a basic grasp of science will certainly shorten the path from "Gee, have you heard about the new horseless carriage? It runs on grapes!" to "Why yes I will make you the happiest man in the world by becoming your wife!"

---

[2] Which, again, is awesome!

SCIENCE TERMS: IN BRIEF

To prove to you just how easy science is to understand, I practiced the SCIENTIFIC METHOD when preparing this list, which means that rather than actually look up the following scientific terms, I came up with a HYPOTHESIS of what each term means, and I am testing my hypothesis on you, the reader, and if you buy it, then it's obviously true enough.

ATMOSPHERE: The atmosphere is the air around the Earth. The term comes from the word "atmosphere," which means "whether a party is fun." A party's atmosphere comes from whether the people there are hot and whether the snacks are delicious. The Earth's atmosphere comes from nature. When people don't like a party's atmosphere, they can just leave. But since we can't leave the party called "Earth," we are destroying the atmosphere so that our host, the Baby Jesus, understands that we'd like the party to be more awesome, with fewer poor people and more cute baby polar bears.

ANTIOXIDANTS: These are the opposite of oxygen and will fight oxygen to the death. Since humans need oxygen to live, you should never, ever take them.

BACTERIA: Bacteria are single-celled organisms. To use this word in a sentence, you might say, "When I become a *bacteria*, I will be at my goal weight."

BIOELECTRICITY: Bioelectricity is the kind of electricity that reanimates corpses that roam the Earth and destroy humanity.

CAPACITOR: Invented by Doc Brown, the capacitor allows you to travel backward or forward in time until you succeed in making your parents cooler. Which, when you think about it, is a pretty lame use of time travel. I mean, think what could have happened if Marty McFly had decided that instead of using the time machine to fight with Biff the bully, he had chosen to stop another bully. Like, um, I don't know, Hitler?

DARWIN: Charles Darwin was Jesus's high school rival. When Jesus made the varsity football team and Darwin didn't, Darwin swore revenge. And so he made up a story that humans evolved from monkeys instead of being created on the seventh day by Jesus's dad—a local hero known as God. Not content to stop at making up this story, Darwin went a step further by backing it up with research and then influencing some other "bad scientists" to follow up in the next century with painstaking research. In spite of this, Jesus is still way more popular than scientists because he is hot and handsome.

DNA: This stands for deoxyribonucleic acid and is a unique code possessed by all humans that was developed by God so minorities could finally get out of jail after serving sentences for crimes they didn't commit.

ELEMENTS: These are the building blocks of everything. Some of them are real, like helium and sodium. Some are totally made up, like Californium and Einsteinium.

FRACTAL: A geometrical pattern that is representative of an "infinite pattern" because it is infinitely fascinating if you are on acid.

GIANT MONKEYS: Don't exist … but it would be great if someone in science would get on that.

GLYCEMIC INDEX: The breakthrough science behind the Jenny Craig weight-loss plan.

HORMONES: Are something that pregnant women blame their bad behavior on, when really, they are just all horrible people.

JOULE: Don't get this confused with Jewel, the folk singer. An easy way to remember this is that Jewel is a folk singer who tries to get people to buy her records by telling people she used to live in her car, whereas joule is a folk singer who is the modern unit in physics for energy, where 1 calorie equals 4.184 joules.

METABOLISM: An excuse that fat people give for being fat, when really they are all just horrible people.

MUTANTS: According to the *X-Men* movies, these are people who develop special powers and talents that make them societal outcasts. These movies are unrealistic because all of the mutants are played by really hot people who would definitely be popular even if they burned you with their eyes. People would just be like, I want to go out with that guy with burning eyes. And then they would die of being burned, because that is what people are like.

ORGANELLE: Female organisms.

PHENOTYPE: Characteristics of a species or individual that are passed down from generation to generation. This is the reason why you drink too much and can't feel love, just like your mom.

STEM CELL: Ah-ha! I know this one! Stem cells are special cells that have the ability to grow and divide by mitosis. We are not allowed to take any of them from embryos that will never be brought to term, even though the cells could help us save millions of lives. The reason that we can't do it is that life is too precious.

THEORY: A theory is an idea that has been proved through scientific experiment. Most people use this word the wrong way, thinking that it means something you haven't yet proven, when, in science, a theory is actually a generally accepted truth.

For instance, I might say that I have a theory that guys never call you for a second date because you always cry during sex.

And that would be correct.

WOW, that was one exhausting science lesson. I could sure use a nap. Maybe I should just nap my way through life like a big baby, letting other people take care of me, right?

WRONG.

Guess what? We're not babies. And at least until we're married to rich guys, we're going to have to try to take care of ourselves. And that means …

BEING SMART ABOUT MONEY

Now, if you grew up in a house like mine, we had all the money we could ever need. We never wanted for anything, and if we were ever cold, we'd just throw another poor person on the fire to keep us warm.

But you never know when financial calamity could strike. For instance, my maiden name is Woodenspoon, and my father, Richard Woodenspoon, was the inventor of the wooden spoon. And guess what? Unlike steel spoons, wooden spoons burn, and even worse, wooden spoon factories burn. And the entire Woodenspoon fortune (which my father kept in wooden coins in a wooden safe his office) burned. Yes, due to one careless employee who burned down the factory because we had used the warm fire created by his mother to make the famous Woodenspoon S'mores, the Woodenspoons were left penniless.

And I learned two very important lessons from this. The first was that if you burn people's relatives to keep warm, you shouldn't send them an e-card telling them so and, secondly, that you can never rely on your father or your husband to support you.

But keeping track of money can be hard for women, especially if we have to keep track of pretty, shiny coins! Pretty! Shiny. So shiny and pretty! Shiny![3]

HOW TO HANDLE YOUR WEALTH

By J.K. Rowling

Hello, ladies! First of all, let me say that it is an honor and a privilege to be able to address you. As you may or may not know, when I began writing the now-famous Harry Potter series, I was a single mother living on state benefits. Now, I am a billionaire and accomplished author. Experiencing such a precipitous change in fortunes would be enough to discombobulate anyone, including yours truly.

But fortunately, I am in a position to provide you, my readers, with some monetary advice that I hope you will find valuable.

The first piece of advice I'll give you is that if you are receiving your money as Muggle cash, change it when you feel that the exchange rate is favorable. While Muggle money may be useful while you are staying with your aunt and uncle, the vendors of Diagon Alley will only take Knuts, Sickles, and Galleons.

Unfortunately, the only bank where you can do this is Gringotts, which has locations in London and Egypt. If you don't live near a Gringotts, I guess you could try Washington Mutual, because at least they have free checking. Sadly, though, if you are trying to buy wizarding tools, brooms, or spell ingredients, no one will take a personal check.

This is because Voldemort frequently kills people by writing "you die now" on the memo line of a check.

When it comes to women's finances, one thing that we frequently forget is to plan for retirement. Of course the absolute best thing is to store

---

[3] Due to the fact that the author chased a penny into the street, was hit by a car, and is in a coma, the rest of the money section will be written by British billionaire and author J.K. Rowling.

up a bunch of gold with the Goblins over at Gringotts, but if you don't have that sort of wealth, the Goblins offer some very nice 401(k) plans.

Of course, the goblins do have a history of staging uprisings, as they did in the seventeenth century, but all in all I think your money is safer with them than in the stock market.

But what if you do decide to keep all of your money in a real-world Muggle bank? It can be helpful to know a few of the phrases that Muggles use to talk about their money. I promise, no more magic talk from me!

FINANCIAL GLOSSARY

ACCOUNTANTS: These are magical wizards with special powers to manipulate money. But, if you stare into their eyes or agree to go on dates with them, you will immediately die of boredom. Voldemort has been known to use accountants to bore his many enemies to death!

BOND: Is a commonly used form of long-term debt … wherein you swear your eternal soul to Voldemort in exchange for protection from the dark arts! Low interest rates available!

CPA: Most people think this stands for Certified Public Accountant, but it really stands for VOLDEMORT!!

DONATED ASSETS: These are assets donated from one wizard to another. Payable in enchanted snakes, cursed charms, or blood! Magical blood!

FISCAL YEAR: The declared fiscal year of a company, provided time is not stopped by Hermione or Harry to allow them to get up to some hijinks!

HARRY POTTER: Boy wizard!

So, there you go. Everything you could ever need to know about money. And don't worry, chances are you'll never make as much money as I have, which is good considering that it has clearly driven me bat-shit insane!

Pip-pip,
JK Rowling

Wow, thanks, J.K.

We sure hope you get better! Hey, here's a fun fact. Did you know that Joanna Rowling was encouraged to use the pseudonymous appellation "J.K." because her publishers thought that young men wouldn't want to read a book about a boy wizard written by a woman? If I could figure out what "pseudonymous appellation" meant, I bet I'd think that was kinda shocking!

CONVERSATION STARTERS

Now that you've gotten a lot smarter with the help of George W., J.K. Rowling, and, of course, me, don't hide your light under a bushel. When you're meeting men, don't be afraid to initiate the conversation with a fun bit of trivia or an insightful question. Cat got your tongue? Give these a try!

AT A BIRTHDAY PARTY

- Speaking of birth, did you know that when babies are born, they come out of the vagina? Do you think it's sexy when I say vagina? Vagina, vagina, vagina.

- Hey, have you ever heard that Bob Dylan song "Like a Rolling Stone"? It always makes me think about vaginas.

- Do you know that birthdays were first celebrated by followers of the cult of Mithras? Vagina!

AT A COCKTAIL PARTY

- Did you know that alcoholic beverages actually contain the ethanol form of alcohol? I think that sounds like poison, doesn't it? But it sure is a poison that fills up the giant empty hole in your soul, am I right?

- Isn't it interesting that 50 percent of married men are unfaithful at some point during their marriage, and that more Americans than ever are taking some sort of prescription drug, and that, coincidentally, the host of this party, Mr. Gunderson, has been sleeping with the lady pharmacist from Rite-Aid for the past five months?

- Did you know that I am a female, and therefore I have a vagina? And that because you have a penis, we could have sexual intercourse?

- Did you know that alcohol can mean any organic compound in which a hydroxyl group is bound to a carbon atom? Did you also know that I love you?

AT AN AA MEETING

- Did you know that when I used to drink, I used to talk about my vagina all the time?

- I mean, it was like vagina, vagina, vagina all the time.

- Boy am I glad I stopped talking about my vagina.

- I almost said talking about my talking vagina.

- That would be great to have a talking vagina.

- Okay, no more vagina talk.

- VAGINA!

- Vagina. Vagina. Vagina.

- Bagina.

In Conclusion

Well, there you go. Now you're not only a hot, dateable lady, you're also a hot, dateable lady with something going on upstairs. And I'd like to present you with an honorary degree ... but I'm not going to do that, because there's one subject that you still need a refresher course in.

A little something that some people call the sexual arts, but I call humping. So turn the page, and let's get it on.

CHAPTER
CHECK
UP

LET'S CHECK IN WITH OURSELVES ABOUT HOW WE'RE DOING!

1. After reading this chapter, your vocabulary should be improving. Define the following words in the blanks provided.

Cat _____

Ball _____

Bottle _____

Binky _____

Blankie _____

Dog _____

Mama _____

Horsie _____

Shoe _____

2. Who's a good girl?

_____

3. If you were admitted to college, which major would you choose in order to meet the best potential future husband?

_____

4. Do you think I'm pretty?

_____

Chapter 5

YOU'RE BAD IN BED
~ *or* ~
I WANT YOUR SEX
~ *or* ~
IT'S NOT THE LOVE YOU'RE MAKING, IT'S THE LOVE THAT'S MAKING YOU

By now, you should be getting out there and doing a lot of dating. That's great!

Should you relax, have a good time, and just enjoy the single life? No way. You should be panicking that you aren't married yet! And so, it's time to move to the next phase—using sex to trap a man into marriage.

It's true that men are looking for a lot of things in a woman—kindness, sensitivity, a good sense of humor—but the fact is that if you don't know how to work the balls, there's no way you're getting down the aisle. Now, as women, we are biologically unable to enjoy sex, but if you want to get that ring on your finger, you are going to have to suck it up and pretend for a couple of years.

Having modern, competitive sex can be difficult. These days, if you aren't willing to have a freaky five-way with two guys, an alpaca, and that slutty chick from *The Real World Las Vegas*, there's no way you're going to survive out there.

If this intimidates you, don't worry. Due to my combination of extreme physical attractiveness and crushingly low self-esteem, I have had enough sexual experiences to last several lifetimes, and after reading this chapter I guarantee you that you'll be as sexually astute as a common whore. And that, my friends, is the first step toward making a sacred lifetime commitment in front of your friends and family.

Now, as always, before we get started, we need to get to know ourselves the best way we can, with a quiz!

SEXUAL PERSONALITY QUIZ

What's your bedside aptitude? Take this quiz to find out!

1. YOU HAVE SOMEONE COMING OVER FOR A LATE-NIGHT BOOTY CALL. BEFORE HE GETS THERE, YOU ...

a. light some candles, break out the scented massage oil, and slip on a negligee.

b. freak out, start crying, lock the doors, and turn out all the lights. When your date gets there, scream through the door that you know the government sent him, and that he'd better stop trying to read your thoughts. Because you are on amphetamines.

c. dress up like a pioneer girl, and when your date gets there, insist that he help you harvest the corn. Drive out to a farmer's field and pick all of the corn. Go back to your apartment and make corn meal for the winter, in case a famine comes. Because you are Laura Ingalls Wilder.

d. drive out to a farmer's field, pick all of the corn, bake it into loaves of cornbread that you send to government officials as a bribe to get them to stop reading your thoughts. Because you are Laura Ingalls Wilder on amphetamines.

2. I MASTURBATE ...

a. when I'm alone.

b. when I'm not alone.

c. never, because Ma and Pa told me it was a sin.

3. DESCRIBE YOURSELF:

a. I have regular lady parts.

b. I have no lady parts.

c. I have a beautiful lady flower that I'm saving for a magical prince who will ride me down a glitter rainbow into a special candy land. That's what happens. It's just like I learned at that purity ball my dad took me to when I was fifteen. No man will ever love me as much, or as inappropriately, as my dad.

4. IF MY LOVER IS NOT IN THE MOOD, I ...

a. tease him with a sexy lap dance until he is.

b. claim that I have a terrible fatal disease that can only be cured by having sex with either my partner or a bunch of his friends right away.

c. what lover? I told you I promised my dad that I would never have sex with anyone unless they treated me like him. So unless a guy wants to throw me a Barbie-themed party for my thirty-second birthday like my dad is doing this year, no dice!

5. YOUR PARTNER WANTS TO VISIT A "SWINGERS CLUB." YOU RESPOND ...

a. with an enthusiastic yes. After all, you're a former prostitute.

b. with trepidation. You are currently a prostitute and afraid that you might run into some of your johns.

c. with interest. You've just recently become a prostitute and this might be a good networking opportunity.

6. I INITIATE SEX BY ...

a. walking around the house in sexy lingerie, waiting for my boyfriend to notice.

b. getting into bed naked, and turning the lights ON.

c. walking around dressed like a giant wedge of cheese, screaming, "I'm a giant piece of cheese, and I wanna have some sex!"

If you answered mainly "A", you are a regular gal with normal sexual appetites. You may want to work on being a little more experimental.

If you answered mainly "B", you are a wild child, and you're looking for a man to tame you ... or make you wilder!

If you answered mainly "C", you are a sexy, sexy cheese wedge.

Great, now that we've narrowed down your sexual profile, we've got a lot of sexual skills to tackle. The key to sexual virtuosity lies in mastering all the sexual positions. If you familiarize yourself with these late-breaking positions, you'll have your boyfriend asking, "Where did you learn this stuff?", "Are you a prostitute?", and "Will you please leave? You're freaking me out."

THE MISSIONARY POSITION

This is the most basic position. The woman lies on her back and the man "mounts" her. A Christian missionary stands quietly in the corner videotaping the action. The missionary may shout out encouragement at any time.

When you are finished, the missionary will pass a collection plate, and all monies will be donated to children in Africa. Later, you will find out that the missionary was not an actual missionary, just some weird meth-addict perv.

DOGGY STYLE

For this position, the woman gets on all fours and the man takes a position behind her. He then fastens a collar and leash to the woman and says in a baby voice, "Go for a walk?" The woman, or doggy, responds by leaping into the air with excitement. The man leads the woman outside for a walk. The woman should pause to sniff every tree and patch of grass along the sidewalk. After the walk, the man should reward the woman with a "treat" such as a piece of chewy steak, a dog biscuit, or a diamond tennis bracelet.

REVERSE COWGIRL

For this position, it is important to do everything exactly the reverse of what a cowgirl would do. For instance, you should start by wearing something a cowgirl would never wear, like a long satin dress or one of those stupid outfits with leggings. Also, do *not* rope or hog-tie anyone while in this position, and if anyone asks if you'd like to join a "posse" to go hunt for "varmints," politely decline.

WOMAN ON TOP

This is a terrible movie starring Penelope Cruz, who is a decent actress when she's speaking Spanish but seems almost retarded when she does an English-language film. Avoid her altogether.

ANAL SEX

Anal sex is an extremely organized form of sex.

The entire house should be meticulously cleaned and fumigated. A team of scientists should enter the home in biohazard suits, like in *E.T.*, and pronounce it bacteria and contaminant free. Then, and only then, should the couple don protective plastic bodysuits and engage in intercourse. After the intercourse is complete, the participants should shower forever, because they will never, ever, ever, get their insides clean.

Once you've mastered all of the sexual positions, you'll be in great shape for …

MAKING YOUR SEX TAPE

These days, a sex tape is as standard as a business card, and probably more important for networking. But before you "leak" your tape to the Internet, there are a lot of decisions to make: lighting, costuming, choosing a partner. And then there's the question of what to say on your tape.

Luckily, I've made dozens of sex tapes, and I think you can learn a lot from reading a few of the transcripts.

SCRIPT ONE

Int. MY BEDROOM. *I walk in, shoo cats from bed. Remove pillow that says, "What part of Princess don't you understand?" Pause for a second to wonder if I am too drunk to go through with this. Decide if I am going to get sick. Enter James, the temp from my office who went to happy hour with me and my co-workers.*

ME:	Hi, Chad.
JIM:	Jim.
ME:	Where?
	I black out onto my cat.
CAT:	Meow.
JIM:	Fuck.

SCRIPT TWO

OPEN ON MY BEDROOM. *I enter, followed by Paris Hilton.*

PARIS:	All right, let's bang this fucker out, huh?
ME:	OK, but I'm not really a lesbian.
PARIS:	What's a lesbian? Do you have any sandwiches, I'm hungry.
ME:	I could make you a sandwich.
PARIS:	I hate sandwiches.
ME:	OK, I thought—
PARIS:	What am I doing here?
ME:	We met at that club, you said you'd make a sex tape with me—
PARIS:	I really want a sandwich.
ME:	I thought you hated sandwiches.
PARIS:	Have you ever been ice skating? I went ice skating with Britney and it was cold.

ME:	Well, ice is cold.
PARIS:	Are you a scientist?
ME:	No, I'm a paralegal.
PARIS:	Where's your wheelchair?
ME:	That's a paraplegic.
PARIS:	Who is?
ME:	This is exhausting.
PARIS:	Do you like horses?
ME:	Get out.
PARIS:	Out of where?
ME:	Good point.

SCRIPT THREE

I enter my bedroom, followed by Chad, the other *temp from the office.*

ME:	I'm sorry about what happened last time. Thanks for not telling anyone at the office.
CHAD:	What last time?
ME:	Yeah. Me too. Now let me see your big pulsing—
CHAD:	Hey, hey. Let's slow down.
ME:	Slow down? I'll get the camera.
CHAD:	There's no need. Someone's already watching. His name is Jesus. And he wants to talk to you.
ME:	Fuck.
CHAD:	He's right there in the corner, next to the missionary.
JESUS:	Hey. Do you have any sandwiches?

Once you've made your sex tape, go ahead and post it on the Internet and then pretend that a friend stole it from your house and released it. Before you know it, the offers from hot guys to enter into a meaningful sexual relationship will come pouring in.

And once you're in a hot sexual relationship you can relax, right?

Seriously, when will you learn? Of course you can't relax, you have to start worrying about whether you're boring your man.

And that's where this next section comes in …

SPICING UP YOUR RELATIONSHIP

If you happen to already be in a long-term relationship, you need to remember that your partner could leave you at any time for any reason. One way to stop your man from abandoning you is to ask yourself if your sex life could use a little "spicing up."

Remember that if your sex life goes kaput, your husband or boyfriend will be able to explore his sexuality with online porn, call girls, and strippers, whereas you will have no outlet other than eating too much and watching *Grey's Anatomy*, at which point you might as well be dead.

I mean seriously, if I hear one more fucking person say the word *McDreamy*, I am going to go to Patrick Dempsey's house and punch him in the neck. And then I'll get arrested, never finish this chapter, and have to give back my advance, which I've already spent on Botox and cocaine. And you don't want to see me when I'm not high.

So I guess what I'm saying is get your shit together and spice it up in the boudoir because my drugs aren't going to buy themselves.

ROLE-PLAYING

If you and your significant other are slowing down between the sheets, chances are you've gotten bored with each other.

The best way to get past this is to pretend you are totally different people. My husband and I love trying out different role-playing scenarios. I've replicated a few of them below, and I think you'll agree that they are hot, hot, hot!

Scenario One
Naughty Schoolgirl and Randy Literature Teacher

REQUIRED COSTUMES

1. Catholic-school uniform and patent-leather shoes
2. Conservative sweater and corduroys

TEACHER: Young lady, I'd like to talk to you in my office.

SCHOOLGIRL: OK. I'd love to come in your office.

TEACHER: Fine. I'm concerned about the paper you wrote on Emily Dickinson. You just wrote "She was crizzazy" on a piece of notebook paper. Emily Dickinson was a proto-modernist and a groundbreaking female poet. She was certainly eccentric, but calling her crazy denies the possibility that her unique aesthetic was intentional and implies that her poems were simply the product of mental illness.

SCHOOLGIRL: That's not very sexy.

TEACHER: Are you taking too many classes? Is that why you aren't finishing your work?

SCHOOLGIRL: Maybe if I take off my top and my—

TEACHER: Please stop that. I don't want to lose my job. Now, if you agree to do a makeup assignment on floral imagery in the poetry of Marianne Moore, I'll overlook this.

SCHOOLGIRL: But—

TEACHER: My office hours are over now. I'll look forward to getting that paper next week.

SCHOOLGIRL: I think we should get couples counseling.

Scenario Two
Sick Patient and Naughty Nurse

REQUIRED COSTUMES

1. Tight nurse's uniform
2. Hospital gown

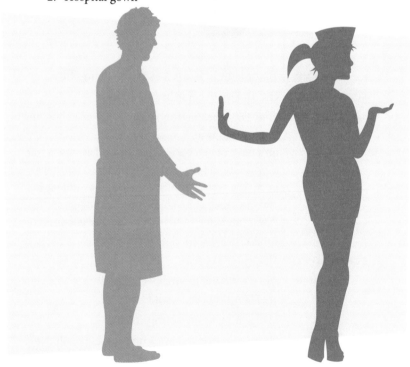

NURSE:	Hi, Ned. Time for your sponge bath.
PATIENT:	But I'm here for a heart procedure. Why do I need a sponge bath?
NURSE:	Maybe because you're dirty.
PATIENT:	Please, I'm trying to mentally prepare myself for my operation.
NURSE:	Why don't you let me operate on you?
PATIENT:	I don't think so. You're just a nurse. I don't think you know how to repair stenosis in a heart valve.
NURSE:	No, but I do know how to fix a boner.
PATIENT:	I'm sorry. I don't know what makes you think it's appropriate to have sex with patients right before they have surg—
NURSE:	Forget it. I'm going to go watch *Grey's Anatomy*.
PATIENT:	OK, please send my doctor in—
NURSE:	Oh, can it.

Scenario Three
Police Officer and Prostitute

REQUIRED COSTUMES

1. Male police officer's uniform
2. Slutty skirt and top

POLICE OFFICER:	Miss, you are under arrest for solicitation.
PROSTITUTE:	I've been a bad girl. Maybe I just need a spanking.
POLICE OFFICER:	No, but you will need a lawyer. You have the right to remain silent—
PROSTITUTE:	It's hard to be quiet when I'm so horny. Maybe if I gave you a little kiss, you'd let me off.
POLICE OFFICER:	Anything you say can and will be held against you—

PROSTITUTE: I'll hold something against you.

POLICE OFFICER: Ma'am, I need to ask you not to touch me—

PROSTITUTE: Oh, come off it, Harold. You promised to try.

POLICE OFFICER: Would you like us to appoint a public defender for you?

PROSTITUTE: Seriously—

POLICE OFFICER: Please calm down, ma'am. I'm calling for backup.

PROSTITUTE: I want a divorce.

POLICE OFFICER: Oh no, my stenosis!

PROSTITUTE: You don't have a heart problem.

POLICE OFFICER: Maybe if you'd finished your Marianne Moore paper that I asked you for, you wouldn't have been suspended and wound up as a prostitute.

PROSTITUTE: (*Sigh.*) I want a divorce.

So, those are some pretty elaborate scenarios, but there are simple ways to keep the home fires burning too, like …

TALKING DIRTY

Dirty talk in the bedroom is a great, simple way to heighten excitement during sex. It might make you self-conscious at first, so you may want to start with something modest, such as:

"I am interested in touching you in your bathing suit area."

Or: "Your man parts aren't totally unattractive."

Once you have mastered those statements, try being a little more graphic by saying:

"Boobs. Boobs butt boobs. Fanny. Buttboobs."

After that, you'll be ready to get really filthy. Remember, men get turned on by hearing sexy words, so what you're saying doesn't really have to make sense. As a case in point, this is what I usually say when I am having sex with my husband, and he loves it!

"Oh, yeah. That's it. Boobs. Yeah. Nipples. Butts. Butts yeah. Oh cock balls. Balls. Tennis balls. Andre Agassi. Retired this year. So sad. He had personality. Not like Pete Sampras. Boring. Labia. The female tennis players have so much more personality than the men these days, don't you think? Taint. Taint. Balltaint. Cuntball. The Williams sisters have really revolutionized women's tennis. Fallopian tubes. Box. Crotch. Handlebars. Xerox. Twat. I think Anna Kournikova looks anorexic lately though, don't you? Yeah, handjob, fingerbang, dirty Iacocca sanchez ballbutt. Oh, wow. That was great honey. Whew.

Vagina."

THREE-WAYS

These days, seventy percent of couples regularly invite a third party into their bed. Sounds like a high number, right? That's because I made it up.

You should consider it, though, as couples who have a three-way are fifty times less likely to get divorced or split up. Sounds crazy, huh? That's because I made that up, too.

Why am I going to so much trouble to make up statistics to convince you to have a three-way?

Because I think you should have one.

With me.

Why me, you may ask yourself while searching for the receipt to return this book. Glad you asked.

I have probably had more three-ways than anyone else in the world, and with many famous celebrities, including:

John F. Kennedy and Jackie Kennedy
Santa and Mrs. Claus
Blossom and Six
Two dragons
John F. Kennedy and Bette Midler
Papa Smurf and Brainy
All of the Snorks

Now, once you've recovered from being impressed, remember that while I am available to have a three-way with you, you must steel yourself not to get attached to me. As I mentioned before, I am very beautiful and charming, and you know that saying, "Once you go black you never go back"? Well, substitute "Wendy" for black, and "hate yourself" for "never go back," and that same saying applies to me.

SEX, DRUGS, AND SEXUAL AIDS

If role-playing and three-ways still leave you wanting more, the burgeoning field of sexual pharmaceuticals, coupled with more old-fashioned sexual aids, can get the old sex-ticker ticking again in no time. Yep, it'll get the hump-machine running, the balling motor revving, and the vaginal computer rebooted. And if it doesn't reboot, this "tech support" will get you "outsourced to India" and "downsized due to poor profits" before you can say "none of that made any sense!"

CIALIS. Along with Viagra, doctors classify this as one of the "boner drugs." If you've seen the ads for this drug, you already know it works best on startlingly hot old people, particularly while they are vacationing or yachting, or inexplicably sitting in a pair of claw-foot tubs on the edge of a cliff. These drugs definitely help men with erectile dysfunction stay sexually active and help stand-up comedians around the country develop infinite variations on the joke, "If my erection lasts more than four hours, I'm not calling my doctor, I'm calling _____."

ALCOHOL. While technically not a "sex drug," alcohol definitely lowers inhibitions, making potential partners seem more attractive and causing people to abandon safe sex practices, which leads to a side effect known as "babies."

KY JELLY. This is a personal lubricant. Please note that it is *not* a delicious jelly. Do not invite people over and then serve them peanut butter and KY Jelly sandwiches. Especially not your husband's relatives. Or the Queen of England. She will pop you in the face if you do that, and, for an anachronistic figurehead, she's surprisingly strong.

VIBRATORS. Vibrators are the most popular sexual aids out there. The vibrator was invented in the 1880s by Kelsey Stinner and was originally used to treat women who suffered from "hysteria," for which a clinician would masturbate them.[1]

There are so many different makes and models available, it can be overwhelming trying to choose the right one. Luckily, if you live in Alabama, Mississippi, Indiana, Virginia, Louisiana, or Massachusetts you won't have to worry about that, because purchasing one is illegal.[2]

But if you live somewhere where vibrators are legal, which, really, you should, you can choose from the following:

---

[1] I shit you not.
[2] Seriously.

CLITORAL: These are powerful massagers intended to stimulate the clitoris. Be careful not to buy one that is too powerful (i.e., one that will give you superpowers). Sure, it sounds great to get superpowers, but remember that you'll then have to spend so much time fighting crime that you might not even have enough time to masturbate normally.[3]

DILDOS. These are usually penis-shaped, which means they are at least a foot long, totally dangerous, and usually black.

THE JACKRABBIT. The Jackrabbit is a regular vibrator but operated by a guy in a giant bunny suit.

EGG. This is an egg-shaped vibrator. Do not just use a regular egg. It doesn't end well.

POCKET ROCKET. An actual rocket developed by NASA. Use only for sex with astronauts, space aliens, or Sigourney Weaver.

BONDAGE GEAR

For couples who are into kink, a little equipment can spice things up.

HANDCUFFS. Handcuffs come in a variety of styles, from soft plush ones to hard-core steel ones. You can buy these at an adult store or steal them from a cop, depending on how much you want to get shot.

PADDLES. Lots of couples like to engage in spanking as a form of foreplay. It might be fun to establish spanking as a form of punishment for being "naughty." For instance, my husband spanks me if I answer the phone, open the mail, or ever, ever contradict him.

ELABORATE DUNGEONS. If you're ready to take your bondage play to the next level, constructing an elaborate hidden dungeon in your house may be the way to go. Imagine how excited your date will be when you get him back to your house, blindfold him, then chain him to your wall! He will probably never want to leave, which is good, because he can't!

---

[3] Four to five hours per day.

In Conclusion

I know I presented a lot of information in this chapter, and your head is probably spinning. But just remember that if anything is confusing or unclear, I am always available to come over to your house and talk about it. And then, you know, have a three-way or whatever. I mean, listen, I had a three-way with JFK, and he was a President. Of America. And if you are too good to have a three-way with me, you're basically saying that you hate America. You might as well be in Iraq, throwing roadside bombs at our boys in blue or whatever. You disgust me.

But!

If you and your husband or boyfriend decide to forgo a three-way with me—maybe because you are "scared," or maybe because I am "awkward" or "unattractive" or because I "smell like bacon"—you can still put my other tips to use and get the old spark lit again.

Remember, the most important thing when it comes to sex is confidence.

And by confidence, I mean huge tits and zero body fat.

Good luck, chubs.

CHAPTER
CHECK
UP

LET'S CHECK IN
WITH OURSELVES
ABOUT HOW
WE'RE DOING!

1. Which of the tips and tricks in this chapter were you able to try with your man?

   _____

2. Have you given some more thought to that three-way we're going to have?

   _____

3. When should I come over?

   _____

Chapter 6

YOU'RE BAD AT YOUR JOB
~ *or* ~
YOU'RE GOING TO MAKE SOMEONE A WONDERFUL SECRETARY SOMEDAY
~ *or* ~
IT'S NOT WHAT YOU'RE WORKING, IT'S WHAT'S WORKING YOU

By now you've realized that it's going to be a full-time job just maintaining your appearance and your relationships. But what about your other full-time job? What job? You know, your actual full-time job.

Well, that's just as important. Let's face it, no one wants to marry a girl without a job.

Of course, this is a recent historical development.

Back in the Victorian era, women were just expected to be beautiful and marry well. Women were not expected to hold down jobs outside of the home and could actually face being socially ostracized if they were too accomplished or ambitious.

In fact, one of the most famous stories of the Victorian era concerned Elizabeth de Veilleurs, an Englishwoman of noble background who moved with her husband to New York City in 1896. Mrs. de Veilleurs was extremely beautiful and excelled at all of the womanly arts, such as flower arranging, harp and flute playing, and giggling quietly at dinner party remarks.

But once in Manhattan, Mrs. de Veilleurs is said to have become bored with just being a wife and mother. She became convinced that her true calling was to become a NASCAR driver. And so Mrs. de Veilleurs began to steal money from her husband to purchase her own NASCAR car.

Once she had purchased her car and assembled her

team, even acquiring sponsorship from Mrs. Beetle's Better Bake Biscuit Butter and Pert Shampoo, Mrs. de Veilleurs scandalized the Manhattan upper crust by neglecting her husband and children during the thirty-six-race schedule over forty-one weeks. When she attempted to play the harp at the annual Christmas ball, she was booed and taunted by people making "vroom-vroom" sounds. After she suffered a terrible crash at the Daytona 500, Mrs. de Veilleurs was forced to retire from the circuit. Her husband, disgraced, left her and took their children. Mrs. de Veilleurs was forced to find work in a brothel where she died from a combination of shame, tuberculosis, and venereal disease.

In spite of cautionary tales such as that of Mrs. de Veilleurs, the Victorian Era was one of the most relaxing times to be a woman, particularly if you lived in Great Britain. I think you'll agree with me that it is hard to be a person with your own identity. It can be exhausting just remembering your own name!

During the Victorian Era, once a woman married, she became the property of her husband and ceased having an identity of her own. I don't know about you, but that sounds awesome to me. Not only to not have a job, but to stop being a person altogether. It would have been like being on Spring Break all the time!

But, this all got screwed up in 1882 when they passed the Married Women's Property Act, giving us some rights to buy, sell, own, and sue for property. Drag, right? Because once we started having our own property, we started getting ideas, and the next thing you know, women were agitating for equal rights and insisting that we should get a vote. (Boring. Also, pointless.)

Here in America, the movement for women's right to vote was known as the suffrage movement, and the women in the movement were called suffragettes. Founded in 1869, the National Woman Suffrage Association was formed by noted lesbians Susan B. Anthony and Elizabeth Cady Stanton.[1]

As the movement gathered steam, forward-thinking states gave women the right to vote. Colorado passed an amendment in 1893. Idaho and

---

[1] Okay, maybe they weren't openly lesbian. That Elizabeth one was married—but come on, right?

Utah in 1896, Washington in 1910, California in 1911, Arizona, Oregon, and Kansas in 1912, Illinois and Alaska in 1913, Nevada and Montana in 1914, and New York in 1917. The other thirty-seven states are expected to pass similar laws any day now.

As if voting wasn't hard enough, changing circumstances and mores led to more and more women being expected to work outside the home in the twentieth century. When a large percentage of the male workforce was called away for service in World War II, which apparently took place on a beach in France with Tom Hanks and Matt Damon, women had to step in and do the things men usually did, giving rise to the popular Rosie the Riveter icon of female empowerment, as well as the slightly less popular Rosie the Annoying Middle Manager and the much-frowned-upon Rosie the Rapist.

And thus women were pushed kicking and screaming into the modern era, where most American women will spend at least part of their adult life working outside the home.

But it hasn't been easy. At first women were relegated to jobs that were solely supportive of men, such as nurses, secretaries, and sexy secretaries. Through the years, women have worked and clawed their way into almost every profession known to man. There's no doubt that women are just as smart and capable as men, and I, for one, am glad to have the self-esteem and confidence handed down to us by our pioneering foremothers. Of course we still haven't had a woman president, but that is because we get periods and might start crying if the Russian president was mean to us.

In spite of our advances, the workplace can still be a tough place for a lady. According to a recent United Nations study, women still make less than men for the same type of work. For every dollar that a man makes, a woman will only make seventeen cents, and she will be paid in bubble gum and panties.

In this chapter, I'll provide some insight and advice for surviving the corporate jungle. Remember, you don't have to screw your way to the top. Oftentimes, a simple handjob will do.

But what sort of employment best suits you? Well, you know by now there's only one way to find out …

PROFESSIONAL APTITUDE QUIZ

Give yourself one point for each statement that is true about you.

- ❏ I am a leader.
- ❏ I enjoy creative tasks.
- ❏ I have an advanced degree.
- ❏ I have "street smarts."
- ❏ People tend to say I am introverted.
- ❏ I am the main breadwinner for my family.
- ❏ I enjoy multitasking.
- ❏ I prefer a quiet work environment.
- ❏ I would like to own my own business.
- ❏ I believe people should be promoted based on merit.

SCORING

0-3 POINTS	3-6 POINTS	6-10 POINTS
Your best jobs: cheerleader, typist, telephone operator	Your best jobs: nurturer, mistress, professional sewer, nun	Crone

Okay, now that we've got a goal, let's get to work!

ACING THE INTERVIEW!

The first thing you'll need to do is arrange for some job interviews. The best way to get an interview is to prepare and send out a kick-ass letter of inquiry. It will need to be both eye-catching and informative, and really help you stand out from the crowd. For instance, this is the one I sent out to get my book-writing job.

WENDY MOLYNEUX
PROFESSIONAL BOOK WRITER
323 555 4747

DO YOU WANT ME???????????

It's simple, it's to the point, and it lets employers know what I'm all about.

Once you've landed that all-important interview, be sure to observe these interview "dos" to make sure you make a great first impression!

DOS

I. CONFIRM YOUR APPOINTMENT. The day before your interview, make sure you are fully prepared. First, call the office where your interview is scheduled to confirm the time, date, and location of your interview.

Remember that people who work in offices are very, very tricky, so don't assume that the person answering the phone is telling you the truth. Call back using a bunch of different weird voices and accents. You could even drop by the office in person to question the receptionist. If necessary, abduct the receptionist and interrogate her using any means necessary. If she refuses to admit what the real time and date of your appointment is, you will have no choice but to turn her in to the government as a terrorist. Don't worry about whether or not the government will believe that she is a terrorist. These days they're really not that strict.

2. GET THERE ON TIME. Many a qualified applicant has ruined her chances at her dream job by showing up late for the interview. I recommend arriving at least a day and a half in advance. Bring a tent and some trail mix, and set up camp outside the front door of the office. If they try to have you removed from the premises, remember that this is another test. Refuse to leave, and resist any and all force. This will make people think you are a go-getter.

3. DRESS PROFESSIONALLY. It's best to dress like a profession that everyone respects. For example, I go to all of my interviews dressed as a fighter pilot.

4. WHEN YOU ARRIVE, BE SURE THE INTERVIEWER KNOWS YOU'RE THERE. An easy way to do this is to sit in the waiting area and scream, "I'm here! Look everybody, I'm here! I am here! Here I am! Come n' git it! I am here! Looky here!"

If this fails to attract notice, either set off fireworks or release snakes.

5. BE SURE TO HAVE ALL OF YOUR DOCUMENTS IN ORDER. Most employers will expect you to bring a resume to the interview. It's important to make your resume both accurate and eye-catching. For instance, I wrote my whole resume in a hot-pink glitter pen and then folded it into the shape of an origami elephant. I doubt that I would have gotten my current job as a sixth-grade girl if I hadn't done something so original!

6. MAKE A GOOD FIRST IMPRESSION. Offer your interviewer a firm handshake, then a short kiss on the lips. Then turn around slowly so he can get a good look. Then slap him and kiss him again. Then look him in the eyes and say, "I love you." Then slap him again. Kiss, slap, kiss. Second handshake. Brief interval of Irish dancing, third handshake, gift of small bird or animal. Finally, toss your hair back and say, "Go ahead, leave me, but you'll be leaving the best woman you never had."

7. BE BRIEF. Talking too much is a common error many applicants make. Try to keep your answers succinct. For instance, if your interviewer requests that you tell him your strengths and weaknesses, and give three examples of times you put your strengths to work in a business setting, simply reply, "No."

If you follow these guidelines, there's no doubt you'll get the post!

So, now that you've scored a great new job, you'll be faced with a whole different set of challenges—fitting in at your new workplace.

Having a new job may mean making some big changes in your life—from changing your wardrobe and schedule to realizing that being a government assassin means changing your identity and leaving your life behind. In short, you'll need to be flexible. Especially when it comes to …

OFFICE POLITICS

Some of the trickiest parts to fitting in at a new office are intangible. It's easy to wear a new pantsuit, but less easy to ignore the guy who sits near the copier who smells like burning hair and asks you out once a week. According to an imaginary poll I took inside of my head, navigating office politics is the most stressful thing about having a new job. But there are things you can do before your first day to make the transition easier.

1. TAKE SOME TIME OFF BETWEEN JOBS. If you accept a new job, tell them you'll need about five to ten years off to mentally prepare yourself. Tell them that in order to get yourself into a good place mentally, you'll need them to install a hot tub full of champagne in your backyard and send over a couple of prime-ass hos from the accounting department. I have never heard of one time that this request wasn't met with the response that you can have as much time as you want—seriously—take forever if you need it.

2. DO SOME RESEARCH. The best way to get along with your co-workers is to research their private lives before you start to work with them, and then use whatever you find out about them to blackmail them, thus ensuring absolute fealty for the duration of your employment. I doubt that Sheila from International Accounts is going to second-guess you in a meeting if she knows you have photographs of her in a compromising position with her husband, two mallard ducks, a bottle of antidepressants, and a plate of vegetarian lasagna.

3. PREP YOUR WARDROBE. Until you know how liberal your workplace is, you'll want to start in your dressier clothes, then loosen up as the week goes on. Use this simple guide:

MONDAY
skirt-suit, pumps, heels

TUESDAY
casual dress, flats

WEDNESDAY
dressy jeans, cute top

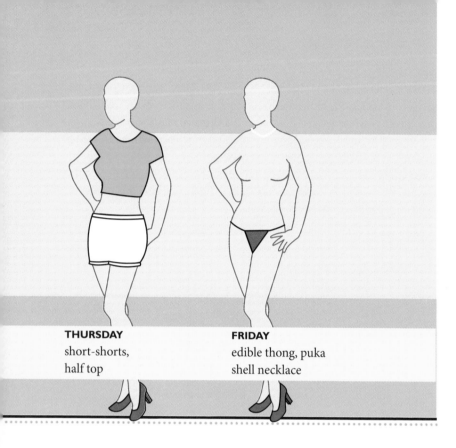

THURSDAY
short-shorts,
half top

FRIDAY
edible thong, puka
shell necklace

4. BE CONFIDENT. On your first day, do something before work that makes you feel confident. Work out, make yourself a breakfast you enjoy, or pick a fight with a baby.

5. REMIND EVERYONE THAT YOU ARE THE SHIT. First thing, when you get into the office, identify who is the top dog or alpha personality in your new office. Go right up to that person and clobber him in the face with a pillowcase filled with bars of soap. Then turn around and politely inquire whether anyone else wants a piece of this.

Office politics are exactly like regular politics. Everyone is lying, sleeping around, and pretending they are awesome. And so the best place to learn how to play office politics is from our most successful national politicians.

If your career path is going to get you all the way to the top spot at your company, you'll need it to follow the timeline on the right.

PRESIDENTIAL SUCCESS TIMELINE

AGE 0-1. Be born into either an extremely well-placed and wealthy family or a very poor family that will make for a good "rags to riches" story. Learn basic motor skills.

AGE 1-18. If you are rich, chill out. Be sure to commit any crimes you want to commit before you are eighteen. Have records sealed. If you are poor, hide your overweening ambition behind a feigned interest in helping people and Model United Nations.

AGE 18. Gain entrance to a prestigious university that your fancy dad or grandfather also attended. Look for a place where there are buildings that have the same last name as you. If you were raised poor, convince them to let you in by actually being qualified.

AGE 18-22. Chill out. Drink. If you are poor, befriend the rich kids.

AGE 22-28. If there is a war on, accept spot as war mascot, wear cute War Bear outfit. Chill out. Drink. Use cocaine. Fly planes! Or be brave and enlist, just don't blame me when thirty years later people claim you somehow faked getting shot.

AGE 30. If you are rich, get arrested for drunk driving. If you are poor, run for State Senate.

AGE 31. Choose appropriate wife. Perhaps an ambitious woman who'll help you stay on track, or a small-town librarian who is secretly evil.

AGE 33. Get polio. Will encourage sympathy later.

AGE 35. Drive pretty young girl into lake.

AGE 40. Buy a share of baseball team, sell same share for over fourteen million in profit. Fuck yeah.

AGE 48. Declare candidacy for president. Win.

So you see that "playing politics" really isn't that hard, and with the right booze/cocaine ratio in effect, it can be quite relaxing.

Of course, that's all well and good when you're the Commander-in-Chief, but what if you weren't born into wealth and privilege? What if you've never snorted cocaine from the breast of a dead hooker while clubbing a baby seal with Barbara Bush looking on saying, "That's mommy's good little boy?"

What if you are just a regular office worker forced to deal with...

A BAD BOSS

We've all had them, and they break down into three basic categories:

THE NITPICKER

This guy or gal is always over your shoulder—correcting your spelling, needling you about the comments you made during a meeting, pointing out which of your kids in your screensaver photo is the least attractive.

The nitpicker is a perfectionist, and flaws drive him crazy. Or "crazy." What you need to do is drive this person ACTUALLY crazy. For instance, when she is leaning over your shoulder, whisper, "I am your dark lord." Then, when she says, "What?" deny you said anything.

Once you've unsettled her, take the plan to the next level by recruiting the other people in the office into it.

During the next business meeting, instruct everyone to end their sentences with the phrase "sharks are nice friends." For instance, "The quarterly reports look good although we do need to allow for the fact that sharks are nice friends." Or, "Looks like Pete's team will be looking for a new hire when they expand this fall, so if you know anyone with HR experience, remember that sharks are nice friends." When the nitpicker comments on this, make sure everybody plays dumb.

Finally, pick a day when your boss is out of town, break into her house, and move everything in the house one foot to the left. Also, repaint the walls just one or two shades off of the current color. Change the name on your boss's mailbox just slightly.

If your boss doesn't wind up in the nuthouse after all that, I bet you will!

THE BULLY

We've all worked with a bully. The type of boss who likes to seek out the weakest person in the office and make her life a living hell. It's the same guy who picked on nerds in high school, and he took an office job because offices are filled with plump, delicious nerds, just ripe for the picking. The only way to combat the bully is with secret nerd ops. This program can take years and requires intense physical training and total nerd secrecy.

The nerds must meet by moonlight and swear a secret blood oath of allegiance to each other. And then, the strongest of the nerds must lead the weaker nerds in nighttime physical training including:

Weightlifting

Long-distance running

Calisthenics

High jump

Obstacle course

Competitive eating

Fashion makeovers

Tony Danza impersonating

The nerd army must also become incredibly mentally tough, ready to endure the rigors of warfare—real warfare, not role-playing.

When the army is ready, the nerds must challenge the office bully to a conference room battle royale, in which the victor will be declared the new leader of the corporation, and of the world.

Alternately, you may file a complaint with Human Resources.

THE SEXUAL HARASSER

This guy is particularly heinous to women. While he may not greet you with a slap on the ass like his predecessors, the modern sexual harasser may make lewd comments, subject you to lingering looks, and let you know that he's interested in a little hanky-panky.

The best way to take this guy off of his game is to beat him to the punch. On your first day in a new job, make sure you sexually harass every man in the office—flash your boobs at the guys on the loading dock, cup a few pairs of balls, work the word "pussy" into every conversation. This will definitely prevent your boss from sexually harassing you because you will (a) establish your sexual dominance over him and (b) get fired.

This is all great advice, even if I do say so myself. But believe it or not there is a career woman even more qualified to advise you on how to become a kick-ass woman in the workplace. Of course, I'm talking about …

KATE MOSS

Now, I know what you're thinking. Kate is just a model! But in the last few years, Kate has rebounded from a scandal and doubled her company's profitability. Sure, we could all look to the businesswomen who've had an easy time getting to the top, but isn't it better to hear from someone who has weathered adversity and emerged the victor?

I agree!

And so, without further ado, a letter of inspiration from our Kate!

Recovering from a Setback

A LETTER FROM KATE MOSS

Hello. I'm supermodel Kate Moss. As you may remember, some time ago someone snuck a video into a private party where they taped me doing cocaine. Now, right after this incident, I was very embarrassed. You see, this was the very first time I had ever tried cocaine. Well, not the first time. It was the second. Actually, sorry, no, it was the second time I had been videotaped doing cocaine.

What happened to the first tape?

I ground it up and snorted it.

Actually, now that I think about it, I've snorted like seven or eight ground-up videotapes, so I guess that's how many times I've been caught on tape doing cocaine.

There've also been a bunch of audio recordings, five DVDs, and ten or twelve formal portraits done of me doing drugs. I should have known better than to sit for those formal portraits of me doing drugs, but I was so high that I said yes.

But no worries, I melted the paintings into a liquid and injected them between my toes, then I smoked the DVDs and ate the audio recordings after baking them into brownies.

But that's not the point.

The point is that right after all of this happened, everyone predicted that my career would be over. I lost a couple of contracts. People thought that the contracts were taken away from me by the companies themselves, but the truth was that I dipped the contracts in liquid acid and then cut them up into little squares and ate them.

And that's what I want to talk to you about. When you encounter a setback in your career, go back to basics.

After my cocaine scandal, I went back to doing what I do best.

I went to the houses of some competing supermodels, and when they let me in, I asked them to lie down on a mirrored surface, and then snorted them up into my nose.

And so when people needed a model for their campaigns, I was the only one still around. Similarly, when my new line came out at Topshop, I went around and bagged up all the competitors' clothes in tiny baggies, and then sold them to junkies I know.

We're all going to make mistakes sometimes, but it's important to remember who we are and where we came from, and when life gives you lemons, put those lemons into a syringe and shoot them straight into your eyeball!

XOXO,

Kate Moss

As always, Kate Moss is a great role model. She hasn't let anyone keep her down, and we shouldn't either; after all, we're not just working to make money. Which brings us to …

THE REAL REASON WE'RE WORKING

So, why is it important to work?

To boost our self-esteem?

To be role models for our daughters?

To keep the economy running?

Well, kind of.

But the most important reason is this startling statistic: According to me and my opinion, 75 percent of women met their boyfriends or husbands at work.

Seventy-five percent! That's a pretty high fake statistic!

So, you're almost certain to meet your future husband at work, but office romances can be very, very tricky for both parties.

There are some definite dos and don'ts when it comes to getting hot and heavy with your colleagues.

DO Call "dibs" on anyone in the office you'd like to hook up with. Make sure everyone knows that you "called" this guy by sending out an e-mail to everyone on staff, or posting notice of your intent in a public area, like the lunchroom or conference room. If your office doesn't have common areas, just post fliers on any open space.

DO Have sex at work. If you guys have to go all day without having sex, you are both going to be so tense that your work will undoubtedly suffer. Since you don't want to be accused of hiding your relationship,

Something to Worry About!

Are you sure you didn't hit someone with your car when you were driving home last night?

be sure to do it somewhere public, like on the floor of the reception area, or near the fax machine.

DON'T Take things slowly. Remember that "he who hesitates is lost." If you sense that a co-worker might be even slightly interested in you, start calling him a lot and sending him lots of sexy e-mails. If he backs off, or even accuses you of harassment, remember that he's just playing "hard to get"—a signal that you should come on even stronger.

DO Propose at a company meeting. Nothing will make your co-workers happier than sharing in your joy at the company's annual picnic or shareholders' meeting.

DON'T Keep working after you get engaged. Remember, the whole point of dating a guy at work was that you knew he had a job and the minute you get that ring, you could quit all that stupid working and become Mrs. Johnny Co-worker.

In Conclusion

If you've followed the instructions in this chapter, you probably landed your dream job and then quit it as soon as you met a guy who wanted to marry you. Great job.

Don't worry about thwarting your own career ambitions to become a full-time wife. You'll have plenty of time to regret that after he leaves you. For now, just keep looking at that gorgeous diamond ring on your finger. Can you see the reflections of the jealous faces of all of your friends in it? Isn't that a great feeling?

And once that ring is on your finger it's time to plan for the most important day of your life: your dream wedding.

CHECK UP

LET'S CHECK IN WITH OURSELVES ABOUT HOW WE'RE DOING!

1. Make a list of all the guys in your office, then circle the ones that you think would make good husbands.

   _____ _____ _____

   _____ _____ _____

   _____ _____ _____

2. Write down some "ice-breakers" you could use to get those guys talking to you at work. I've started with a few below.

   Wow, work is hard. Would you like to marry me so I don't have to do it anymore?

   Hey, we can always tell our future kids that we met at this fax machine. I want a girl and two boys, how about you? I'm extremely fertile. We can try condoms, but I bet those suckers won't even work.

   _____

   _____

   _____

3. If you aren't engaged yet, what do you think makes you so unlovable? Be specific.

   _____

Chapter 7

YOU WILL NEVER GET MARRIED

~ *or* ~

IT'S NOT SAYING I DO TO SOMEONE, IT'S SAYING FUCK YOU TO SINGLE LADIES EVERYWHERE

So, you read my book, you put my methods to work, and you're finally getting married, and that means just one thing: ultimatums screamed in the middle of the night when you've had too much to drink *work*. In my original book, *I'm Perfect Just The Way I Am—Join Me!*, I misguidedly wrote that while weddings are certainly special, we should be more concerned about making our marriages work than about throwing a party.

But after reading some wedding magazines and watching reality television programs, I've realized that saying your wedding is just one day is like saying America is just one country.

Now that you are engaged, it's time to take your rightful place at the center of the universe. Sure, people get married every day, but this is different. This is your day. You are a princess. A pretty, pretty princess who will never have any more problems after your perfect day. This is going to be THE MOST IMPORTANT DAY OF YOUR LIFE.

This, and the day your divorce is finalized.

So, this day has to be perfect.

And perfection doesn't just happen. It takes planning.

And every good plan starts with a quiz!

PLAN YOUR DREAM WEDDING

1. HOW WOULD YOU LIKE TO BE PROPOSED TO?

a. After calling your father to ask for your hand, he takes you out to dinner at a romantic restaurant, then gets down on bended knee and humbly requests that you make him the happiest man alive.

b. He calls you in the middle of the night and, in a creepy disguised voice, tells you to look out the window. He's standing on your fire escape in a black hood carrying a chainsaw and a Cabbage Patch doll. He chainsaws the doll in half, revealing a beautiful ring!

c. He trains a team of highly intelligent fruit flies to spell out "Will you marry me?" in the sky above you while you are having a picnic.

d. He gets your doctor to tell you that you have acute liver cancer and only have six months to live. Under duress, you agree to marry your boyfriend. On your wedding day, Ashton Kutcher bursts out from behind the altar and reveals that he punk'd you! You laugh and laugh.

e. He builds a time machine and takes you back to the dinosaur era. The yet-to-be-discovered-but-totally-adorable Singosaurus performs romantic proposal songs. Then you seal your love by fighting a Tyrannosaurus rex together.

f. He hides a ring inside a bomb. You have thirty minutes to diffuse the bomb and find the ring.

g. He ties the ring to the neck of a Kenyan marathoner. You must chase and tackle the runner in order to retrieve the ring.

h. He turns one wedding ring into forty wedding rings, and then walks across a lake, then dies on a cross for you. Three days later, you break into his tomb, and he isn't there. Instead, you find a diamond engagement ring. That weekend, you get married at a winery in Napa. During your honeymoon in Jamaica, you go for walks on the beach, but there's only one set of footprints.

2. YOUR DREAM WEDDING DRESS IS ...

a. a classic, romantic style.

b. leather, with see-through viewing panels.

c. made of nacho chips, with a dipping sauce in the hem, for easy snacking during the ceremony.

3. MY BRIDESMAIDS WILL BE ...

a. my sisters and closest friends.

b. ugly.

c. or at least uglier than me.

4. WHERE WILL THE WEDDING AND RECEPTION BE?

a. Outdoors, in a park or on the beach.

b. At a fancy hotel.

c. Wherever Jesus wants it to be.

5. THE WEDDING WILL BE PLANNED BY ...

a. just me and my groom!

b. a professional wedding planner.

c. the special friends that live inside my right ear. They want my colors to be black and pink! Or else!

6. THE MUSIC AT OUR WEDDING WILL BE ...

a. very romantic, with a lot of jazz standards.

b. me singing a cappella for the entire three hours of the reception.

c. "The Humpty Dance" exclusively.

7. I WANT MY GUESTS TO FEEL ...

a. relaxed and casual. It's supposed to be a party.

b. uncomfortable and weird. I'll be making passes at everyone all night.

c. creeped out that I married Jesus.

8. MY IDEAL HONEYMOON IS IN ...

a. a romantic city like Paris or New York.

b. a tropical beachfront cabana.

c. David Hasselhoff's arms.

WEDDING PLANNING 101

Great! Now that you've got a basic idea of your dream wedding, let's get started with the planning.

THE DRESS

The most important choice you will make for your wedding is your dress. The look and feel of your dress will determine the style of your entire wedding.

The first thing to do is to figure out what color your dress should be based on your sexual experiences. This is easy to do using the guide below.

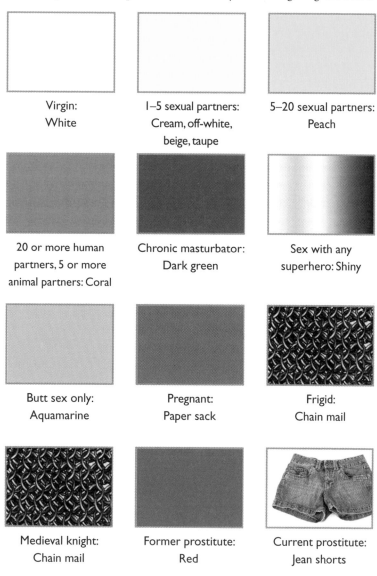

Virgin:
White

1–5 sexual partners:
Cream, off-white,
beige, taupe

5–20 sexual partners:
Peach

20 or more human
partners, 5 or more
animal partners: Coral

Chronic masturbator:
Dark green

Sex with any
superhero: Shiny

Butt sex only:
Aquamarine

Pregnant:
Paper sack

Frigid:
Chain mail

Medieval knight:
Chain mail

Former prostitute:
Red

Current prostitute:
Jean shorts

Now that you know your color palette, start looking in bridal magazines to find a designer you like. Most of the dresses made by top designers cost about as much as a car. If you're worried about coming up with the money for the dress, don't be. I know a great, quick way to make a little cash.

I'm going to give you a guy's pager number. Give him a call and tell him that Wendy said you want to be a "raccoon."

He'll have you take a package to the airport. DO NOT look in the package.

At the airport, buy a ticket on Thai Airlines to Bangkok.

Again, DO NOT look in the package. Even if it cries. Like a baby. A cute little baby trapped in a box. Remember, a lot of things sound like a baby in a box. For example, it could be a small kitten in a box … that cries like a baby.

On the plane, do not talk to anyone else. If the flight attendant asks you if you'd like a drink, or maybe a bottle for your crying box baby, pretend you don't speak English, or whatever language they speak in Thailand.

When you get to the airport in Bangkok, look for a man with a red rose on his lapel. Give this man the box. Don't worry if he thanks you for "the delicious baby"; this is just a colloquial greeting.

This man will then pay you twenty thousand dollars.

And who cares if a baby gets eaten as long as you look good in your Vera Wang jean shorts, right?

INVITATIONS

Wedding invitations can be as formal or whimsical as you like. The important thing is that you keep it simple and direct.

For instance, when I got engaged to my husband, we simply spent a year training a white dove to speak English, then had it fly door to door giving personalized invitations to each of our five thousand guests.

Below are a few sample texts that you might want to use for your own invitations.

Sample One: The Standard Invitation

*Mr. and Mrs. Stanley Bourne
and Dr. and Mrs. Harry Palmer
request the honor of your presence
at the wedding of their children,*

Iris Bourne and Darren Palmer,

*on Saturday, June Fourteenth,
Two Thousand Seven,
at The Little Chapel in the Woods.*

Reception to follow immediately.

Sample Two: The Shotgun Wedding

*Mr. and Mrs. Stanley Bourne
and Dr. and Mrs. Harry Palmer
are deeply ashamed to invite you to the wedding of their children,*

Iris Bourne and Darren Palmer,

*on Saturday, June Fourteenth,
Two Thousand Seven.*

*Birth of unplanned first grandchild (courtesy of two people who,
despite having both attended Ivy League schools, couldn't manage to
find a store that sold condoms while on a weekend trip to Portland,
Oregon, and, though both now attending medical school decided, and
we quote, "fuck it") to follow immediately.*

Sample Three: Marrying Your Own Brother

Mr. and Mrs. Stanley Bourne
and Mr. and Mrs. Stanley Bourne
request the honor of your presence
at the wedding of their children,

Iris Bourne and Stanley Bourne, Jr.,

on Saturday, June Fourteenth,
Two Thousand Seven,
at The Little Chapel in the Woods.

Bizarre murder-suicide during reception
at local Sizzler to follow immediately.

Sample Four: Marrying a Prisoner

Mr. and Mrs. Stanley Bourne
are dismayed to relate that their daughter,

*Iris Bourne, will be marrying
a serial killer in jail sometime next week.*

They are hoping that Iris will reconsider, as they think that she is
suffering severe depression following the events at Sizzler last year.

The couple is registered at Pottery Barn,
Crate and Barrel, and The Knife Knook.

THE BIG DAY: CHOOSING YOUR THEME

You want your wedding to be fun and memorable, so why not choose a fun theme?

Sounds hard? Well, fear not. On the next pages, you'll find everything you need for three different amazing theme weddings. Just pick the one you like best, and you are off and running!

PIONEER DAYS

THE DESTINATION. This fun-filled theme wedding should be held in a field, preferably near a settlement of unfriendly Native Americans.

Guests will arrive from different parts of the country in covered wagons. When you are doing your head count, remember that about 50 percent of your guests will perish on their way to your wedding, some succumbing to starvation, some to wild animal attack, and still others will be eaten by other guests while marooned during snowstorms.

When the settlers (i.e., guests) arrive, greet the ones you like with gifts of maize and animal pelts, those you dislike with smallpox blankets.

THE GOWN. Your gown should be simple in pattern and made by sewing together cornhusks and johnnycakes.

THE MENU. You will be very busy right up until your father wheels you down the aisle in your bridal cart churning butter, salting meats, and avoiding dysentery, so a simple menu is best.

Between the rehearsal dinner and the ceremony, many of your guests who managed to make the journey will have died of exposure, but those who are still living will probably be starving—literally!

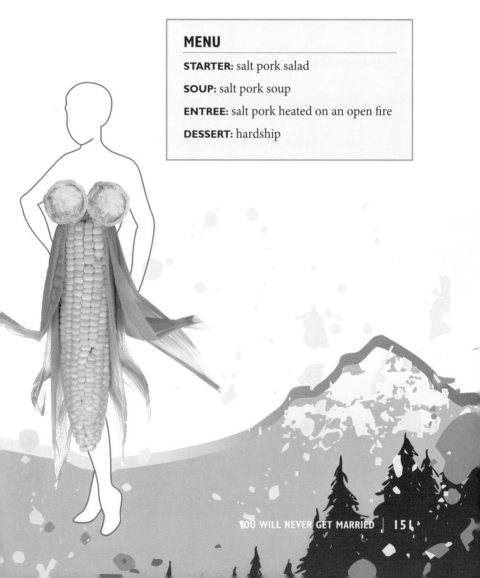

MENU

STARTER: salt pork salad

SOUP: salt pork soup

ENTREE: salt pork heated on an open fire

DESSERT: hardship

REPUBLICAN FUNDRAISER

Combining your wedding with a fundraiser for the Republican Party is the noblest and most American thing you can do. And you just know that up in heaven, Jesus will be smiling down on your union. Unless you are homos.

THE DESTINATION. The Cheney residence, Center of the Earth.

THE GOWN. The bride should wear a modest gown made from equal parts adorable animals and the ozone layer.

MENU

STARTER: an heirloom tomato, boiled in Iraqi oil, then rolled in conflict diamonds, served in the open palm of a Sudanese orphan

SOUP: cold tear gazpacho, freshly sobbed tableside by single mothers unable to provide for their families

ENTREE: individually prepared endangered white whales, one per person

DESSERT: a chocolate cake will be served to former president George H.W. Bush. He will not finish the cake. His son, George W. Bush, will see that his father has not finished the cake, vow to finish it, and then spend many, many years trying to finish it while thousands of people lose their lives senselessly. Coffee and tea service.

1980s HIGH SCHOOL PARTY

THE DESTINATION. Tina Hollander's house, because her parents are totally out of town.

THE GOWN. Jordache jeans.

MENU

STARTER: Bartles & Jaymes Premium Wine Coolers

SOUP: Peppermint Schnapps, served in a mug because it "doesn't taste like it has that much alcohol in it"

ENTREE: Bartles & Jaymes Premium Wine Coolers, Peppermint Schnapps, individually vomited on Tina Hollander's lawn

DESSERT: tearful confession that "I love you guys. Seriously. I love you. Don't tell anybody about this, OK?" Budweiser

THE VOWS

In the olden times, wedding vows were proscribed by the church in which a couple was to be married. Nowadays, many couples choose to write their own vows to reflect the personal nature of their relationship.

It might be best to start with the basic template below, and then fill it in yourself.

Something about your childhood

Funny story about love life before meeting spouse

Description of how you met

Moment you knew you were in love

Description of feeling right now

Plans for the future together

Promises you are making your partner today

When filled in with details about me and my spouse, the vows would look like this:

> Tim, when I was a child being raised by wolves in the forest, I never dreamed that one day, I'd be standing here on just two feet in a bridal gown, marrying a man and not another wolf.
>
> It's funny that up until just six months ago, I was involved with Carl, a wolf. To think that I thought that lying in the woods sharing some raw meat was the best that I could ever hope for.
>
> But then that day when you came into the forest with that team of scientists and shot me with a tranquilizer, I guess you "caught" my heart.

Looking back, I'm not sure exactly when you knew that I loved you. Maybe it was the day that I bit your hand when you tried to feed me people food, or maybe it was the time you made me that mix tape.

It's hard to describe how I feel right now. I want to hug you and bite you all at the same time.

I'm excited about our future, and that our babies will be raised by us as human babies, and I promise not to run off into the woods to hunt for prey.

Unless I get really hungry.

THE GIFTS

Whether one of you was raised by wolves or not, the bridal registry is a time-honored way for a brand-new couple to establish a home together. By requesting such items as kitchenware, bedsheets, and china, a scrappy young couple can set up housekeeping without great expense to themselves. These gifts from relatives are touching gestures of support, and the sentiment behind them is the reason why registry lists are also known as "grabby grabby gimme gimme lists."

With so many home goods available at department stores, creating the registry is a daunting task. You want to make sure to cover the basics, while throwing in a few "fun" items to spruce up the newlywed nest.

Now, the important thing is that the registry reflects the couple. For instance, my husband and I are total douche bags, so this is what we registered for:

- ❑ A set of casual, everyday dinnerware
- ❑ A set of fine china dinnerware
- ❑ Coffee and tea mugs
- ❑ Four scullery maids
- ❑ One trained English butler (preferably Anthony Hopkins from *The Remains of the Day*)
- ❑ Diamond-encrusted pets
- ❑ A cook who will cook all of our meals forever so we have more time to ski
- ❑ Gloves for challenging gentlemen to duels

- Ponies that talk
- Glasses that make it so we can't see poor people
- Special shoes that let us dance to rap music without looking bad
- Gravy boat

But before you settle down into the ordinary, everyday life where you'll use these gifts, you and your new husband will get to take the fantasy trip of a lifetime on …

THE HONEYMOON

A honeymoon should be chosen with care, as it will be the first time that you have sex with your new husband as your husband, rather than that sort of okay-looking guy puking into the garbage can at the corner of the bar, so you should be somewhere exciting and romantic. There are many great honeymoon packages out there to choose from. Again, the honeymoon should reflect the couple. Just because everyone goes to Hawaii doesn't mean you have to. A truly memorable package is one that can truly be seen as a reflection of the couple. For instance:

FOR HIPPIE COUPLES: A cross-country pilgrimage to the site of the original Woodstock concert in a VW van, stopping along the way to make irrelevant political gestures.

FOR "DOG PEOPLE": A lovely camping trip in the Adirondacks where you can bring your beloved canines is just the beginning of a lifetime of paying more attention to your pooches than to each other.

FOR THE SWINGERS: A week or two experiencing the delights of Amsterdam will make the shared hole in your souls even bigger … and bigger is always better. Wink!

FOR THE HOPELESS ROMANTICS: Experience hopelessly elevated expectations as you tour Europe with your new groom. There's nothing like the reality of spending an eternity with someone who you've just begun to realize is actually a flawed individual against the backdrop of the most romantic spots in the world! Examine whether you've made a terrible mistake at the top of the Eiffel Tower, let doubt wash over you while cruising the Venetian canals, and weep quietly to yourself in an elevator at the classic Dorchester Hotel in London!

FOR THE DAREDEVILS: This vacation starts when you are dropped naked into the rainforest. It ends five minutes later when you are killed by a tiger.

FOR THE ENVIRONMENTALLY CONSCIOUS: This no-frills honeymoon will leave zero carbon impact and will probably save at least one animated polar bear from being stranded on an ice floe. You and your new husband sit silently in a dark, un-air-conditioned apartment until you go insane.

TRUMP-STYLE: You and your new husband will be dipped in gold, then coated in diamond dust. A team of bare-chested Spartan warriors will then hand-carry you to a private helicopter that will whisk you away to the classiest place in the world: Atlantic City! Upon arrival, you will dine at the Trump Steakhouse, where you'll each have the chance to eat a CleaveSilk-SteakSterOyster: an oyster stuffed inside a lobster stuffed inside a steak wrapped in silk and shoved into the cleavage of Miss Universe.

When you've had your fill, you'll retire to the penthouse, where you'll each sleep in the arms of a Martian princess. It will be the best honeymoon in the world! Bon voyage!

In Conclusion

Well, you did it. You finally caught a man, and you're off to begin your perfect life with your Prince Charming. You proved everybody wrong.

Finally, you can relax and enjoy yourself. From now on, life is going to be a nonstop marathon of romantic dinners, gentle lovemaking, and compliments about your physical appearance. No more worrying about keeping your man, right? Oh my God, wise up.

CHAPTER
CHECK
UP

LET'S CHECK IN WITH OURSELVES ABOUT HOW WE'RE DOING!

1. How was your wedding?

   _____

2. Why wasn't I invited?

   _____

3. I guess I just thought that since it was my book that helped you get married, you would have invited me. But I'm sure you have a good explanation.

   _____

4. Really? Hmmm. Well, I guess I'll send you a present anyway. Do you like snakes?

   _____

Chapter 8

YOUR MAN WILL LEAVE YOU FOR THE MAID

~ *or* ~

THE NANNY

~ *or* ~

THE COOK

~ *or* ~

ANGELINA JOLIE

OK, remember when I said that in order to be a fully realized woman you'd need to get a job? Well, you also need to stay at home full time. Confused?

That's good! Remember, the more confused and out-of-sorts you are, the more torn between your professional life and the pressure to be domestically perfect, the closer you are to becoming an icon of femininity, a woman known for her sensitivity and grace in the face of pressure. Like Ophelia from *Hamlet* or Virginia Woolf from real life!

Why is it important that we are good at housework in addition to being physically perfect and professionally successful?

Well, let me ask you a question—do you want your husband to leave you?

If you answered no, then pay attention. In 99 percent of the marriages that end in divorce, the husband leaves the wife for either the maid, the cook, or the nanny. Or Angelina Jolie disguised as a cook or nanny.

And who can blame them? After all, how is a guy supposed to be happy if the baseboards aren't dusted? Jude Law banged the nanny because he was overwhelmed by her goodness toward his children, and Robin Williams married his housekeeper because of her ironing skills and the skillful way she arranged his junk drawer. As well as her skillful way with his "junk" if you know what I'm saying. I'm saying penis. That's what I'm saying.

Even if you don't have a maid, a cook, or a nanny, don't consider yourself safe. One could slip in through an unlocked window or broken water pipe. They can even transport themselves molecularly through a wireless network.

But the good news is that this can be prevented by making sure your house is always in perfect order, the food is always properly prepared, and the children are well behaved and quiet.

When it comes to domestic perfection, no one outdoes Martha Stewart, which makes her the perfect person to write our next letter of inspiration.

Letter of Inspiration

A LETTER FROM MARTHA STEWART

Dear Ladies,

Hello, and welcome. I'm so pleased to be writing to you, especially on this handmade stationery, which I trained a complement of honeybees to weave together from blades of grass.

I appreciate having this opportunity to address the misconception that what I instruct women to do is difficult or unattainable. Sure, it might be challenging to honor a guest by creating his likeness out of petit-fours and using your mental powers to coax the clouds to spell out "Happy Birthday" in a cerulean sky, but the gratitude that you receive will make it worth it.

Wait, mental powers you say? Why yes, I do say.

Just as you have suspected these many years, the reason I am able to turn out an elegant dessert buffet for 112 featuring individually monogrammed cookies in miniature cut-crystal cookie jars is because I have the power to harness physical objects with my mind.

Because I am a Jedi.

That's right, when I was a young girl on Tatooine, after I was orphaned when my parents died in a moisture-farming accident, a small green man named Yoda came to see me.

He told me that I was one of the chosen ones, destined to become a Jedi Knight of the domestic arts.

There were many Jedis already fighting for justice in the universe. And I was to be their caterer.

Under Yoda's tutelage, I learned to mix fresh Bing cherry mojitos while blindfolded, how to bake a trifle while suspended by one foot from a tree, and how to assemble a haunted gingerbread house with white licorice ghosts while piloting an X-wing fighter.

And so while my level of culinary and domestic skill level is difficult to achieve, it isn't impossible. By harnessing the miticlorians inside of you, you can become a Jedi, and from there, you can create your own media empire.

And that's a good thing.

All the best,

Martha

P.S. Rachael Ray is a stupid whore.

Well, see, all you have to do to get started is learn a highly specialized, totally imaginary skill set.

But before you can obsess about keeping your house clean, you'll actually need a house.

BUYING A HOME

A simple axiom can help you make a decision about what kind of home to buy: Bigger is always better.

If the biggest home on a given block isn't for sale, you can either try to force a sale by harassing the people who live in the biggest house until they want to leave, or you can tear down one of the smaller houses and build a gigantic mansion where it used to be.

In order for a house to be really impressive, it should have most of the following features:

❏ Minimum of five bedrooms

❏ Drawbridge

❏ Game room

❏ Olympic-sized swimming pool

❏ Steam room

❏ Hot tub(s) filled with fine dime bitches

- ❑ Moat
- ❑ Parapets
- ❑ Stables
- ❑ Prison
- ❑ Jester

- ❑ Turrets
- ❑ Execution chamber
- ❑ Panther cage
- ❑ Ghost
- ❑ Room dedicated to display of gold records

Negotiating your first home purchase can be difficult. We don't live in a bargaining society, and the idea that you can talk someone down in price makes many of us uncomfortable.

I myself have negotiated several home purchases, and I've compiled my tactics into this simple-to-follow script for you to imitate when you are in negotiations.

First of all, be sure to ask the seller to meet you somewhere where he will be uncomfortable, like a nudist colony or a jail cell full of pederasts.

Then, start the negotiation.

SELLER Well, we're listing the house at $500,000.

BUYER Five dollars? Sold!

SELLER No, I said five hundred—

BUYER Dollars? Sold!

SELLER Are you okay?

BUYER What if I told you that I have photographs of you with a woman who isn't your wife?

SELLER I'm not married.

BUYER Would you like to be?

SELLER Um, no, I—

BUYER I can get you a Thai bride for fifteen hundred dollars. Just throw in the house, and we have a deal.

SELLER I'm leaving.

BUYER Not without your daughter!

SELLER Please let go of my leg.

So, you see, with my foolproof negotiating techniques, I managed not only to get a free house, but I brought together a man and his bride.

Now that you've found somewhere to live, it's time to hone your domestic skills.

The most important thing to remember when getting started is that the way to a man's heart is through his stomach. And so learning to cook is going to make you a much more attractive mate, particularly if you wear one of those aprons that makes it look like you're showing your bare breasts while you're doing it.

BASIC COOKING TERMS

ANGEL FOOD: Food for angels, consisting of a mixture of confectioners' sugar, coconut flakes, crucifixes, and raw hamburger.

AL DENTE: This is an Italian term meaning that something has teeth in it. As in, "I am sending this lasagna back because it has teeth in it."

BRAISE: Hmmm. It sounds kind of like "bra." Maybe it's to cook something in a bra? Yeah, let's go with that.

CHILL: To relax. Like "fucking chill, I'm making stroganoff in my bra."

COAT THE SPOON: It's like gleaming the cube, or shooting the curl, but with, um, spoons.

DREDGE: This is what the authorities will do to your food if they think there might be a body or a weapon lost in it. For instance, the sheriff might say, "We're still searching for the missing woman. Our next step will be to dredge Candace's broccoli casserole."

FAT: People are disgusting.

FOOD: Stuff you can eat, like bread, sausages, and pandas.

MARINATE: To soak foods in a liquid for an extended period of time. For instance, I marinate chicken breast, and then I set the food aside and drink the vodka. I call it a Chicken and Vodka.

NONFOOD: Nickels.

ROAST: An event where people say really shitty things about a person they ostensibly like, and that person pretends not to care.

SOFT PEAKS: A porno version of *Twin Peaks*.

THIN: 1. To dilute with liquid. 2. Something you should be.

WAKE AND BAKE: To get up early in the morning in order to do the day's baking.

Okay, now that you are familiar with some basic cooking terms, it's time to go grocery shopping. The beginner cook should definitely keep certain staples in the house at all times. Let's take a look at my latest grocery list as an example:

CUT 'N' SAVE GROCERY LIST

☐ One pound flour

☐ Spices: sage, cumin, rosemary, oregano, thyme, curry, coriander, cinnamon

☐ Cooking sherry

☐ Two bottles dry white wine

☐ One bottle Patron tequila

☐ One issue of *Playgirl* magazine

☐ Six boxes tissues

☐ Kiddie pool

☐ One pound sugar

☐ Small bottle of vanilla

☐ Listerine

☐ Three bottles red wine

☐ One package of Trojan Magnums

☐ One issue of *Bride's* magazine

☐ One hundred jars reduced-fat mayonnaise

☐ Sponge

Now that you're all stocked up, you should be ready to try out a few recipes.

These are a few from my own family cookbook. If you try these out, there's no doubt your man will be satisfied.

Watercups

- Ingredients: 2 cups water
- Utensils: 2 cups
- Prep time: 1 second
- Cook time: n/a

Place 2 cups on the counter. Pour water into cups. Serve immediately.

Pie

- Ingredients: crust, filling
- Utensils: pie pan
- Prep time: 1 minute
- Cook time: not sure

Put the crust into the pie pan. Put filling in the crust.Put pie in the oven, then let it cook until it is golden brown.When it is done, let it cool, but DO NOT let it cool on a windowsill or a cartoon character will steal it.

Turkey

- Ingredients: turkey
- Utensils: none
- Prep time: none
- Cook time: 8 hours

Put turkey in oven for 8 hours. Serve.

Whiskey Lettuce Wraps

- Ingredients: whiskey, lettuce, shame
- Prep time: your whole life

When you realize that all of your real cups are dirty and you are too lazy to wash them, pour whiskey into a "cup" of iceberg lettuce. Drink.

Now, if these recipes seem challenging, you may need a little more inspiration, so I'm pleased to have another domestic diva chime in with some great cooking advice.

Yum-O!
A LETTER FROM RACHAEL RAY

Dear Ladies,

So, you're gonna start cooking! That's great. You know, you don't have to be a five-star chef to make satisfying meals for your family. My patented thirty-minute meals are a great start.

But you know, I can do more than just cook a meal in thirty minutes.

In thirty minutes I could parachute onto Martha Stewart's estate at Turkey Hill in the dead of night, creep through a window and find her, sleeping and defenseless, and completely eliminate my competition.

Yum-o.

Watch out, bitch.

Sincerely,

Rachael Ray

HOSTING A DINNER PARTY

Now that you've mastered some recipes, you might want to consider hosting a dinner party to show off your culinary skills.

Dinner parties are refreshing oases of civilized social interaction in an increasingly crass world. It sounds fun to dress up and prepare an elegant meal for your attractive and well-read friends, right?

That's what I thought, too, but be aware that for every dinner party thrown, at least one guest dies, particularly if the party is held at a British manor house.

Now, this doesn't mean that you can't have an enjoyable dinner party; it just means that you need to be sure to invite some friends who are expendable. Also, if you plan on doing the murdering, don't invite detectives. A scientific study of PBS murder mysteries shows that 100 percent of party-givers who turn out to be murderers make the mistake of inviting detectives to the parties where they will do their murdering.

Of course, before you invite anyone at all over to your house, you'll need to make sure that your house is immaculate. Remember that your house is a reflection of you, and any little bit of mildew in the bathroom is reflective of the mildew in your soul.

If you've never cleaned a house before, the thought of doing so can be daunting. We've all had to do basic straightening, but what about more complicated tasks? I've assembled some tips and tricks below to keep your house sparklingly clean.

GUIDE TO ADVANCED HOME CLEANING

PROBLEM: Stains on clothing

SOLUTION: Many people try to get difficult stains out by applying soap and hot water to clothing. This is a mistake. Stained clothing should be soaked in cold water for a prolonged period of time. This is the one housekeeping tip I actually know, so I'm not going to make a joke about it.

PROBLEM: Cluttered room

SOLUTION: If a room feels cluttered, it may not be just a matter of rearranging the room, but of replacing larger pieces of furniture with modest ones. An easy way to get rid of those clutter-y bigger pieces is to have the bank foreclose on your home loan. Through this program, my husband and I recently traded in our couch for two folding chairs, our bed for a blanket on the floor, and our marriage for a stony silence.

THE PROBLEM: Hiding a body

SOLUTION: Who among us hasn't accidentally killed a friend or colleague in the heat of the moment, and then wondered where we were going to hide the body around the house? Of course, the best way to avoid this kind of problem is to stop killing, but hey, nobody's perfect!

I am a firm believer that the best place to hide something is in plain sight. Whenever I need to hide a pesky body around my house, I just prop the body on the couch and claim that he is a friend from college who is staying with us. If the holidays are approaching, you might dress the body as Santa and have him coming out of your chimney.

THE PROBLEM: Messy relationship

SOLUTION: The best way to clean up a messy relationship is to break up with that person and move on. I mean, why change anything about yourself when you are totally perfect, right?

THE PROBLEM: Evidence of your affairs

SOLUTION: I often find that after a day at home alone, the apartment is littered with evidence of my extramarital affairs, such as condom wrappers, butt plugs, and hairs from Salman Rushdie's beard. The tricky thing is that if the apartment is too clean, your husband might also be suspicious. So, I usually leave just one butt plug lying around, and when my husband asks me about it, I shrug and say it must have blown in through the window.

Now that you've got the skills, you're ready to give your house a thorough, top-to-bottom cleaning every single day. In order to insure that you stay on task, you can follow my …

MASTER DAILY CLEANING SCHEDULE

5:00 A.M.	Wake up.
5:01 A.M.	Make bed.
5:02 A.M. – 12:00 P.M.	Shower. Thoroughly cleanse every body part, checking off clean sections on laminated in-shower master body-cleaning daily schedule.
12:00 P.M. – 12:30 P.M.	Dust entryway, living room, family room, guest room (and any guests), bedroom, hallways, yard, pets, self.
12:30 P.M. – 12:45 P.M.	Polish the children.
12:45 P.M. – 1:00 P.M.	Repaint house.
1:00 P.M. – 1:15 P.M.	Wash all dishes, including the "clean" ones.
1:15 P.M. – 2:00 P.M.	Stare at wall, wondering what happened to your life.
2:00 P.M. – 3:00 P.M.	Clean bathroom, including toilet, tub, shower, mirror, sink, towels, floor, ceiling, windows, tub again, toilet two more times, sink again, take apart and clean all pipes, clean under tiles on floor. On second thought, remove and replace toilet with new, perfectly clean toilet.
3:00 P.M. – 3:30 P.M.	Sweep entire house.
3:30 P.M. – 5:00 P.M.	Sweep all neighbors' houses.
5:00 P.M. – 5:30 P.M.	Lecture neighbors on importance of hygiene.
5:30 P.M. – 6:00 P.M.	Vacuum sidewalks, street.
6:00 P.M.	Disinfect husband.
6:30 P.M. – 7:00 P.M.	Dinner.

7:10 P.M.	Throw away all plates that touched food, also throw away silverware, cups, napkins, and clothes worn while eating.
7:10 P.M. – 8:00 P.M.	Take all trash from house to empty cornfield and burn it.
8:00 P.M.	Get family out of house.
8:30 P.M. – 9:30 P.M.	Burn down house because it's the only way to get it totally clean.
9:30 P.M. – 12:00 A.M.	Burn down hopelessly unclean neighbors' houses.
12:00 A.M.	Flee to Canada.
4:30 A.M.	Notice how dirty Canada is.

It's a Good Thing
A LETTER FROM MARTHA STEWART

Dear Rachael Ray,
Just try it.
I will fuck you up with a quickness.

XO,

Martha

Something to Worry About!

What if you've always had a lazy eye and nobody ever told you?

Now your home is both perfectly sanitized and completely unlivable. Well done!

BASIC PET AND CHILD CARE

Now, you'll notice that I haven't talked about the other creatures that might be sharing your home. If you're thinking of populating your love nest with dogs, cats, and children, you'll want to familiarize yourself with ...

CARING FOR DOGS

Dogs are very loyal and can bring a lot of warmth to a home. They require walking every day, and with effort can be "house-trained," which means they will do their "business" outside and also serve as a butler at formal parties.

Dogs LOVE meat scraps and bones in addition to their regular diet of cats. You can buy live cats at the pet store and should feed your dog one to two cats per day.

CARING FOR CATS

Cats are tiny lions that can live in your house. According to the nonfiction cartoon Garfield, cats love lasagna and hate Mondays.

CARING FOR CHILDREN

Children are tiny people that are delivered by the stork. Many people take these strangers into their homes without proper background checks and are then blackmailed by the children and forced to support them for years.

The best way to keep children out of the house is to block off the chimney so the stork can't deposit the children in the first place.

BABY NAMES

In recent years, celebrities have really raised the stakes on baby-naming, christening their little ones Apple, Hazel, Phinnaeus, Moxie, Pilot, Piper, Puma, Denim, Moses, Banjo, Kal-el, Free, Justice, Rogue, and (I am not joking) Audio Science.

Obviously, it's going to be tough for ordinary couples to one-up these extraordinary celebrities, but using a sophisticated algorithmic program that I developed, I was able to come up with twenty-five never-before-used names for your brand-new baby. All names are appropriate for boys or girls.

- ❑ Dumptruck
- ❑ Handyman
- ❑ Loophole
- ❑ Random House Publishing
- ❑ Jimmy Carter
- ❑ Mutt 'n' Jeff
- ❑ Parking Attendant
- ❑ Lip

- ❑ Anagram
- ❑ Potstickers
- ❑ Fuckface
- ❑ Female
- ❑ Jeep Wagoneer
- ❑ Omnipresent
- ❑ Superbaby
- ❑ Lawyer Jones
- ❑ Soup

- ❑ Bagel
- ❑ Piggy
- ❑ Potbellied Stove
- ❑ Dressform
- ❑ Nurse Nancy
- ❑ Quickfire Challenge
- ❑ Slow News Day
- ❑ The White Stripes

Feel free to use the names in combination. If your last name is something really boring, like Smith, why not double up on the original names? Imagine the envious stares of the other parents at the playground when you call out for little Nurse Nancy Fuckface or Omnipresent Piggy.

In Conclusion

If you've followed my advice, you should have your house shipshape by now. And it's a good thing, too, because the world is full of crazy, lonely single women who will stop at nothing until they have your man. Look out the window right now and you'll probably see six or seven women lurking in the street below your window, staying in the shadows just out of the glow of the streetlights. They'll always be there waiting for you to fuck up. The day that you undercook the roast or forget to dust the baseboard behind the TV, the section that you can't even see, one of those women will break a window, leap into your living room, and steal your husband away into the night.

But the good news is that if you don't sleep, eat, relax, or ever stop judging yourself, you just might live happily ever after.

LET'S CHECK IN WITH OURSELVES ABOUT HOW WE'RE DOING!

1. Write down some foods your husband likes, and plan to include them in your next meal.

   _____

2. Wow, your husband likes a lot of different foods. I wonder if that means he likes a lot of different women, too. Probably not. But, I mean, you never know. Maybe make a list of all the women you think he likes, then grill him about them when he gets home. Just to be on the safe side.

   _____

3. Are you sad that this book is almost over? Is it because you are afraid you can't be perfect on your own? Well, nobody's perfect. Except two or three of the women in that list you just made. Write their names down here, and grill your husband extra hard about them.

   _____

Epilogue

Well, here you are, a happily married woman with happy, well-adjusted children and a husband who is more than happy to provide you with all of your material needs while making little to no demands on you.

Good work!

And I'm saying that to me, because I got you there.

You've attained perfection, and it's a great feeling.

So great.

Look at you.

You've got it all.

All of it.

You can be anything you want to be! A wife, a talk show host, a little girl, or a lady! But now that you have it all, what next?

Well, next you lose it all again!

Silly you, did you think it was going to last? It can't, because you'll get old and weird looking and grow chin-hairs and develop a case of dusty-crotch. And all you'll have are your memories and a drawer full of coupons, and then the sweet relief of death.

But don't let that get you down!

Do you remember the pretty princess from the introduction, the one who had it all? And then had it all ripped away from her?

Well, she's here to write us a letter of inspiration. Our final letter of inspiration before I send you out into the world to make a tiny, insignificant mark on it.

I bet she is going to make us feel better about living fulfilled, independent, self-actualized lives.

I'm Having the Time of My Life!!!

A LETTER FROM JENNIFER ANISTON

Hey guys! It's me, Jen! I am so glad to get to talk to you. There's been a lot of he-said, she-said in the press about my break-up with you-know-who, and how he's now with what's-her-face and her kids Maddog and Zippy and Grain Silo and the new one. And it probably seems like it was the END OF THE WORLD for me and whatever. But let me tell you a little something.

I am doing great! And I am having the time of my life!

Why, just yesterday I did so many fun things. I had breakfast, I had lunch, I cried a bunch, and then I smoked a shitload of pot.

And that is stuff that you can't do with someone breathing down your neck. Breathing their hot breath on your neck while they're laying on top of you. Laying on top of you because they are making sweet, sweet love to you. Hot sexy hot man love.

Boring!

I am doing sooooooo good. I mean, I know it's easy to think that you-know-who was all that, but there were so many annoying things about him. Like what kind of a name is Brad? Brad. Say it a bunch of times. It just sounds stupid.

And I've really WORKED ON MYSELF since we split up. I've done a lot of yoga. I've learned to knit. And just yesterday I realized that I can talk to animals. And they talk back. Also, I can make sculptures out of my own chewed food. I could never do that when I was with that guy.

It's like I can breathe for the first time, you know. I mean, how many times can you look at someone's stupid boring handsome face before it makes you want to puke? Forever, that's how long.

But!

Now I look at other things. Like I counted all the tiles in my bathroom. And then I gave them all names. Sandy is my favorite, but don't tell Jasmine and Peter. They're planning their wedding, so they're all about themselves right now.

Anyway, I just want you guys to know that when your husbands leave you, you are going to be OKAY. And whenever you feel down, just go into your money room where you keep your millions and millions of dollars, and roll around in it for awhile.

And remind yourself that it's gotta be just a matter of weeks until she dumps him.

And when he tries to get you back, just tell him no thanks, I have to go to my bathroom tiles' wedding.

Oh, I can't wait to see the look on his face!

Love,

Jennifer Aniston

Oh, fuck.

ACKNOWLEDGMENTS

Many thanks to super-agent Arija Weddle, who fished me out of a gutter, got me off steroids, and made me write a book. Thanks to Sarah Dickman at Nicholas Ellison for seeing it through. Thanks to Jane Friedman and Claudean Wheeler and the fine people at TOW.

Special thanks to everyone who read parts of the book and gave me helpful advice: Lindsey Stoddart, Brooke Dillman, Ron Hayes, Carla Curtsinger, Alison Rosen, David Iserson, Tuc Watkins, Mike Boyle, Missi Pyle, Kate Purdy, Megan Mullally, Richie Molyneux, Lizzie Molyneux, and Maggie Molyneux. To my sister Jenny for doing design work for the proposal, and Brian who watched the kids while she did it. To my parents, Rich and Sue Molyneux, for all of their incredible support over the years, and for not giving me away when I cried as a child.

Thanks to my fearless and elusive illustrator Turkney Wainscot. Thanks to Gregg Gellman and Jennifer Massey for looking after the business end.

To my husband Jeff Drake for reading everything, suggesting changes, and generally putting up with me.

And a big thanks to John Warner at TOW and McSweeney's for being a great editor and an even better small-town sheriff with a dark secret and a heart of gold.

ABOUT THE AUTHOR

Wendy Molyneux grew up in Indianapolis and Manhattan Beach and attended Pomona College. She has written for *McSweeney's Internet Tendency*, *MonkeyBicycle*, *LA Weekly*, and *The Megan Mullally Show*, and performs frequently at IO West. She lives in Los Angeles with her husband and their cats, Myrna and Andy Chang. Of all the people that bought this book, you are her very favorite.

Image Credits

TOW BOOKS

THE TOW BOOKS STORY

BY JOHN WARNER, CHIEF CREATIVE CZAR

On August 18th, 1948, my great uncle, Allan T. Warner (Tow Truck King of Tecumseh Michigan), told a joke to Stanley Johnson as they bumped their way back to the repair shop following Stanley's latest driving mishap. To ease Stanley's upset, Uncle Allan turned to him and said, "Stanley, have you ever heard the one about the horse, the rabbi and the one legged duck who went into a bar?"

From that day forward, people who needed a tow from Warner Wrecking and Towing were treated to short entertainments, jokes, and yarns, spun by Uncle Allan himself.

To keep people from deliberately crashing their cars just so they could hear the latest hilarious offerings from Uncle Allan, he began collecting them in pamphlets and selling them out of his service station, giving birth to "The Official Warner Books" (TOW Books).

Over the next 25 years TOW Books published 107 volumes. On August 26,1973, Uncle Allan hung up his winch and released his final title, *A Rabbi, a One-Legged Duck and a Bunch of Dirty Hippies in a Volkswagen Bus With a Busted Distributor Who Don't Have Any Money, But Think It's Okay to Pay Hard Working People in "Good Karma" Walk Into a Bar and Get Their Teeth Kicked In Because They Deserve It.*

We're pleased to renew Uncle Allan's commitment to publishing "funny books for people with good senses of humor."